The smart saver's guide to protecting
your money and helping it grow

MONEY IN THE BANK

How to Get the Most for Your Banking Dollar

STEPHEN BROBECK

and KENT BRUNETTE

edited by Jack Gillis

A Perigee Book

D1397612

This book is intended to provide accurate and authoritative information on the subjects covered. It is for information and educational purposes only. Neither the publishers nor the authors purport to render legal, accounting, or professional advice of any kind on any of the topics discussed. For such advice, you should consult with an appropriate professional.

Perigee Books
are published by
The Putnam Publishing Group
200 Madison Avenue
New York, NY 10016

Library of Congress Cataloging-in-Publication Data

Brobeck, Stephen.
    Money in the bank: how to get the most for your banking dollar/
Stephen Brobeck, Kent Brunette.
        p.   cm.
    "A Perigee Book."
    Includes index.
    ISBN 0-399-51822-3 (alk. paper)
    1. Finance, Personal. 2. Saving and investment. 3. Banks and
banking—Customer services. I. Brunette, Kent. II. Title.
HG179.B743 1993   93-8370 CIP
332.024-dc20

Cover Design by Mike McIver
Printed in the United States of America
1 2 3 4 5 6 7 8 9 10

Table of Contents

ACKNOWLEDGMENTS

The authors could not have written this book without the assistance of several persons. Stuart Krichevsky, agent at Sterling Lord Literistic Agency, and Steve Ross, senior editor at G. P. Putnam's Sons, helped conceptualize the work. Naphtali Hoffman, an economics professor at Elmira College, coauthored an earlier Consumer Federation of America (CFA) guide to consumer banking services that served as the starting point for the writing of this book. CFA intern Lynda Davis researched specific bank policies on checking and savings accounts. Critical reviews of draft chapters were conducted and information provided by the following persons: Jim Hamill and Carol Reynolds, Federal Trade Commission; Craig Hoogstra and Laura Polacheck, American Association of Retired Persons; Gerri Detweiller, Bankcard Holders of America; Ed Mierzwinski, U.S. Public Interest Research Group; Diane Casey, Independent Bankers Association of America; Phil Corwin and Kawika Daguio, American Bankers Association; Sean Kennedy, Electronic Funds Transfer Association; Peter Gray and Catherine Allen, Citibank; Janet Koehler, AT&T Universal Card Services; Bill Moss and Meredith Layer, American Express; Keith Gumbinger, HSH Associates; and Mike Barrett. Dr. John Brobeck, Jack Gillis, and Steve Ross made valuable editorial suggestions, and Alisa Feingold and Edna Friedberg of Gillis and Associates designed and produced the book. The authors are indebted to each of these persons.

Introduction

Today's Financial Services Marketplace

As a result of numerous changes in recent years, today's banking environment is significantly more complex, confusing, and perilous than that of only a decade ago. And, with the increasing speeds at which banks can fold and new banking products and services enter the market, it is getting even more so by the day. If you are like most Americans, you could probably save yourself both money and heartache by taking a closer look at your banking relationships. Consider the following three questions:

❏ Are You Getting Ripped Off by Your Bank?

In 1990, hundreds of customers at the National Bank of
Washington were talked into converting their certificates of
deposit (CDs) into commercial paper, which represented
stock in the bank, because it commanded a higher rate of return. When the bank failed a couple of months later, CDs
were covered under deposit insurance protection, but the
commercial paper was worthless. People lost millions of
dollars.

In Colorado recently, bank tellers persuaded many older
savers to abandon their passbook savings accounts in favor
of new bank-offered mutual funds. Although they carried
higher yields, these mutual funds also represented higher
risk investments, were uninsured, and were coupled with
administrative charges and fees that were not attached to
savings accounts. After all of these costs were factored in,
the bank's customers would probably have been better off
with their lower rate, insured passbook savings accounts
that they were with the seemingly more attractive mutual
funds. To add insult to injury, the bank tellers were getting
paid a $20 referral fee for each account they switched from
savings into mutual funds.

❏ Are You Confused by the Products Your Bank Offers?

Walk into any Citibank office today and what do you
see? Attractive signs advertising the availability of 650 different mutual funds; "Investment Consultant" booths where
you can buy securities products strategically plopped down
in highly visible lobby locations; posters complete with little
"Wall Street" signs proclaiming that the investment choices
of Wall Street are available at local Citibank offices; bro-
chures hyping tax-deferred annuities, IRAs, CDs, Keoghs,
SEPs, corporate and government bonds, home equity loans,

and various mortgage products; and racks of loan and credit card applications. Ironically, traditional bank products like checking and savings accounts are the least visible among the bank's offerings. Moreover, these promotions are not accompanied by prominent disclosures clarifying the deposit insurance status of the diverse products offered. And the areas where traditional banking activities are performed are not clearly separated from areas where other types of activates take place.

A cautious bank customer in Boston recently was repeatedly assured by several bank representatives that all of his funds were indeed federally insured. When the bank was later taken over by regulators, some $30,000 of his savings was not insured. He then called several other banks in the Boston area, explained how his accounts were structured, and asked them to determine the deposit insurance coverage. Over two-thirds of the banks he called gave him incorrect information!

❑ Are You Spending Money Unnecessarily?

How much does the privilege of plastic cost you each year? To calculate your credit card costs, add up the expenses on all of your credit cards from last year, including the interest and annual fees, plus any additional costs (transaction fees, charges for convenience checks or cash advances, late-payment and over-the-limit fees) you paid. you may be surprised by the total, but you are not alone: the average card-carrying American paid a whopping $450 in credit card interest in 1992. Most people often do not realize that those colorful pieces of plastic are costing them a bundle.

Similarly, do you have any idea how much your bank account cost you last year? If not, you should analyze your bank statements and add up the following: monthly account maintenance fees, ATM charges, balance inquiry fees, monthly statement fees, fees for using live tellers, account reconciliation fees, overdraft charges, interest charges on overdraft protection, stop-payment fees, wire-transfer fees, etc. Upon closer inspection, most consumers are surprised to realize that they are being hit with a variety of hidden costs which can total as high as several hundred dollars a year.

Consumers are encountering all kinds of problems in today's financial services marketplace. In these times when every penny counts, many of us are being victimized by some financial institution practices. That is why it is important to learn how to sort through the confusion of today's environment, protect yourself, cut your losses, and maximize your position.

The Revolution in Consumer Banking

For the past decade, consumer banking has undergone a dramatic transformation. Indeed, banking as usual today means something totally different from what it meant two, five, or ten years ago. A combination of deregulation, heightened competition, and technological change has revolutionized the financial services environment.

Deposit Insurance Crisis. Throughout the 1980s and into the 1990s, solvency concerns wreaked havoc upon the nation and became one of the country's most pressing domestic issues. As The Wall Street Journal reported in early 1993, "more depositors are losing money in bank failures than at any time since the Great Depression." These concerns have created a crisis in confidence in the nation's financial services delivery system. Many of us question the integrity of financial institutions and whether the nation's depository system will be able to respond to our needs. If you are like many others, you may still be worried about the safety of your funds, how to avoid problems, and what would become of your savings should your financial institution fail.

The Consolidation of Banking Institutions. The nature of banking has changed dramatically in recent years. The mergers of major banks, like those of Chemical with Manufacturers Hanover and Bank of America with Security Pacific, along with increasing numbers of smaller mergers, are only the most visible examples of the consolidation trend sweeping the financial services industry. The number of savings and loans has already shrunk from more than seven thousand to fewer than two thousand. The days of the friendly neighborhood bank that is locally owned and operated are quickly disappearing. Highly automated, impersonal megabanks are replacing them. We should all be concerned about the impact these changes will have upon our day-to-day banking activities and what to do if our local institution changes hands. In these days of growing reliance upon centralized office functions often located in a distant state, it is becoming increasingly difficult to locate financial institutions that adequately respond to all of our credit and depository needs.

Banks Increase Income and Profits. Financial institutions are more concerned about their own survival and profitability than they are about their customers' financial well-being. In an effort to squeeze additional income out of their

customers, financial institutions have charged them high
credit card interest rates, lowered the interest rates on savings products, imposed new and higher service charges and
fees, jacked up initial and minimum balance requirements,
and placed more onerous terms and conditions on products
and services. These actions have produced record profits (in
excess of $32 billion in 1992 alone) for the nation's financial
institutions. As banks employ new techniques to enhance
their balance sheets, improve bottom lines, and increase
shareholder profits, millions of unsuspecting consumers
across the country are losing money.

Banks Offer Nonbank Services. In today's highly
competitive environment, many of the nation's banks are
hawking all sorts of goods. Offerings are no longer limited
to traditional banking products and services like checking
and savings accounts, installment loans, credit cards, and
mortgages. They also include insurance, annuities, mutual
funds, and home equity loans. In such an environment, however, consumers are confronted by a bewildering array of
products and services. It is often difficult for most people to
sort through these complex and confusing products.

New Players. Difficult economic times have forced
consumers to search for new ways to keep their heads
above-water. Those lucky enough to have personal savings
have seen their interest rates plummet to historically low
levels. As a result, many people are abandoning lower re-
turn/lower risk products and selecting higher return/higher
risk options. Many consumers are seeking alternative investment vehicles, like mutual funds, brokerage accounts, and
other higher return investments in an effort to shore up sag-
ging yields. More and more, people are looking to sources

outside of banks—securities firms, insurance agents, and diversified financial services companies—for savings and investment products and services.

New Consumer Attitudes. As the country continues to dig itself out of difficult economic times, one thing is certain: Increasing numbers of us have become more cost-conscious. In many respects, America has turned into a nation of bargain hunters. Indeed, many people are seeking out creative ways to avoid or minimize all sorts of expenses in their lives. The timing is now ripe for consumers to focus their attention upon financial costs, which have been quietly siphoning away their hard-earned money.

New Consumer Protections. In recent years, Congress has passed several laws to protect bank consumers. These include the Expedited Funds Availability Act (limits the holds that banking insitutions can place on deposited checks), Truth-in-Savings (requires understandable account disclosures and prohibits certain abusive practices), Home Equity Loan Consumer Protection Act (requires up-front diclosures and prohibits lenders from changing terms after a contract has been signed), and Fair Credit Card Disclosure Act (requires disclosure of annual fee, grace period, interest rates). In addition, several new federal regulations of importance to consumers have recently been implemented. What's more, in recent years, many state legislatures and regulatory bodies have enhanced consumer safeguards relating to various financial products and services. For example, Vermont and Maryland require credit-reporting agencies to give residents free copies of their credit reports. In addition, most states have imposed usury ceilings to protect their citizens against exorbitant interest rates.

Technological Advances. The last decade has also seen
tremendous changes in the delivery of banking services by
computer. Automatic bill payments, computer bill payment
services, automated teller machine networks, debit cards,
and home banking by computer are some of the new com-
puter-based technologies available. Used correctly, these
advances can help you eliminate unnecessary time and effort
spent on many financial chores, enhance your personal
safety and convenience, and save you money. You need to
be armed with the requisite tools to put state-of-the-art
computer know-how to work for you.

In today's complex and confusing financial services marketplace, you can no longer afford to be uninformed or to
trust a financial institution for unbiased advice. You need to
carefully analyze all of your financial decisions. In doing so,
you must be able to see through the hype, hullabaloo, gimmicks, slick promotions, advertising campaigns, and marketing ploys to determine whether you actually benefit from
highly touted products and services.

Money in the Bank helps you sort through the confusion
of today's marketplace, minimize the significant costs of financial services in your life, and maximize your financial vi-
ability. It analyzes all banking options—from checking and
savings accounts to credit cards to home equity and installment loans to electronic banking. In doing so, it identifies
the best deals and provides consumers with a practical
framework for comparing all types of financial products,
services, and offerings.

Chapters 1 through 7 discuss different types of deposit
accounts. Chapter 1 addresses the number-one concern of
consumers with substantial funds in these accounts—ensur-
ing that these monies are safe. Chapter 2 examines different

checking options, including NOW accounts. Chapter 3 introduces and compares a wide range of savings and investment options, which are each discussed more fully in chapters 4 through 7.

Chapters 8 through 10 examine different types of consumer loans available at banking institutions. Chapter 8 explains consumer credit and how to use it. Chapters 9 and 10 discuss specific types of credit, including credit cards, charge cards, installment loans, and home equity loans. First mortgage loans and mortgage refinancing, however, are not included in this work.

Chapter 11 reviews the wide array of available electronic banking services, including automated teller machines (ATMs), direct deposits, banking by computer, and debit cards. Chapter 12 explains how consumers can resolve complaints against banking institutions.

1

Deposit Insurance

Larry is concerned about the safety of funds he has deposited in a financial institution. Like many of us, he needs to know the answers to important deposit insurance questions. What is deposit insurance and what are its limits? Are my funds safe in a state-insured institution? What can I do to protect myself? Do I need to shop around for safe and sound financial institutions? Should I withdraw my money as soon as I catch wind of a possible problem? Should I spread my money around in several different institutions to insulate myself from harm and inconvenience should one of them go under? Could some of the money I have worked so hard to build during the years be lost if the bank I trust goes bust?

Americans have recently experienced a barrage of deposit insurance crises—the savings and loan debacle, problems with state deposit insurance programs, and threats of an impending crisis for commercial banks. You cannot turn on the television, listen to the radio, or look at a newspaper without being subjected to gloom-and-doom reports about the solvency status of the nation's financial institutions. In this troubling environment, most people are experiencing a crisis in confidence in the nation's financial system.

Your confidence, however, will likely be renewed once you understand basic deposit insurance rules and, when necessary, change your investment habits to get the most from your funds. This may take a little effort on your part, but remember, the typical depositor who lost money in a failed institution did so unnecessarily; most losses could have been avoided if depositors had been aware of how insurance rules affected their accounts.

Given their complexity and high tension levels, deposit insurance issues intimidate many people. This need not be the case. By following the series of simple, easy-to-understand steps identified in the "Shopping for Deposit Insurance" section in this chapter, you can make absolutely certain your funds are secure. If your financial institution is taken over by the FDIC, you need to know what to expect, what your rights are, and how to enforce them.

Federal Deposit Insurance Corporation

The Federal Deposit Insurance Corporation (FDIC) is an independent agency of the federal government that insures deposits in 98 percent of the nation's banks and savings and loans. Since most financial institutions in this country qualify for FDIC coverage, the information in this book reflects the FDIC's insurance rules. A similar agency, the National Credit Union Administration (NCUA), operates the National Credit Union Share Insurance Fund (NCUSIF), which insures federal credit unions. NCUA rules normally track those of the FDIC.

The FDIC's purpose is to guarantee the safety of money you deposit in qualifying accounts in federally insured institutions. The FDIC relies upon the Bank Insurance Fund (BIF), the Savings Association Insurance Fund (SAIF), and interest earnings to accomplish its mission. These funds get their money from insurance premiums paid by banks and savings and loans across the country. To assure public confidence in the nation's depository insurance system, both of these funds are backed by the full faith and credit of the U.S. government. This means that whatever happens in the deposit insurance system, the United States government will stand behind the money you place in federally insured institutions (just so long as basic deposit insurance rules are followed).

The FDIC's task is formidable. It guarantees deposits in some 11,700 banks and 2,500 savings institutions across the country. Each FDIC-insured institution must meet high standards of safety and soundness in its banking practices. These institutions are routinely examined by the FDIC and federal and state regulators to assure that these standards are observed. Through these actions, the FDIC tries to make certain that problems are corrected quickly and crises are averted wherever possible. If an insured institution must be closed down, the FDIC will step in to protect depositors up to allowable limits, liquidate an institution's assets, and settle its debts.

Since the FDIC and its actions have a substantial impact

upon you and your financial security, it is important to learn
more about the FDIC and deposit insurance. Spending a
little time and effort on these issues now can save you
money and headaches down the road.

Resolution Trust Corporation

The Resolution Trust Corporation (RTC) is a federal
government agency that was created in 1989 to clean up the
savings and loan deposit insurance crisis. Its purpose is to
protect deposit accounts in insolvent savings and loans (also
known as thrift institutions), to liquidate insolvent thrifts,
and to manage and sell failed savings and loan institutions'
assets. In this role, the RTC helps to contain the cost of the
multibillion-dollar savings and loan bailout and to recover
taxpayer funds. The RTC is also authorized to investigate,
initiate civil litigation, and refer appropriate cases to crimi-
nal law enforcement officials for possible actions against
people whose negligent or fraudulent activities helped contribute to the thrift crisis. The RTC's powers and activities
are similar to those of the FDIC, although its scope is limited to dealing only with failed savings and loans. The RTC
works closely with the Office of Thrift Supervision (OTS),
which is the regulator for federally chartered or insured savings and loan associations.

Shopping for Deposit Insurance

Before shopping for deposit insurance, you should ask
yourself how important deposit insurance protection is to
you. Today, many people have been shocked into the real-

ization that insured products often come with a hefty price tag attached—lower interest rates. Consequently, when scrambling to find the best returns, many people have abandoned lower risk/lower return insured banking products—like deposit accounts or certificates of deposit—and opted for higher risk/higher return uninsured investments—like stocks or mutual funds.

Most people fall into one of the three categories illustrated below:

Lois and Bill want the peace of mind in knowing that their funds are as safe as possible and not ex posed to any risk. They opt for insured products.

Carol and Gary are willing to take greater risks in an effort to reap greater returns. Like countless others, they are flocking to uninsured products.

Christopher and Justin are splitting their money between insured deposits and uninsured investments. This diversification insulates them from some harm, allows them to reap greater returns, and assures that some of their deposits are absolutely safe.

The choice is yours. If you have decided that deposit insurance protection is important to you, read on.

The most stable and secure place you can put your savings is in insured deposits at financial institutions (banks, savings and loans, and credit unions). This is because many but not all of the products offered by these institutions are covered by deposit insurance. Even though the deposit insurance crises of late have weakened public confidence in these institutions, they are still absolutely the best places to put your money if you want the maximum possible protection against loss. All of your insured deposits will be protected (so long as they fall within insured limits—usually up to $100,000). So you can sock your money away in an insured account at a financial institution, rely upon Uncle Sam's guarantee, and rest comfortably.

However, given the uncertainties of the current climate, you need to do more than simply plop your money down at your corner bank. You should take the following five steps to protect yourself and avoid deposit insurance problems.

Step 1: Put your money only in federally insured institutions.

Step 2: Shop around for sound financial institutions.

Step 3: Keep your account balances within insurance limits.

Step 4: Be on the lookout for changes that might affect your coverage.

Step 5: Be sure the products you select are insured.

❑ **Step 1: Put Your Money Only in Federally Insured Institutions**

If deposit insurance protection is important to you, put your money in FDIC-insured institutions. Financial institutions insured by the FDIC are required to indicate their FDIC-insured status in their advertising and must also display an official sign at each teller window or station. If neither of the following signs is displayed at the bank or savings and loan where you have an account, beware! Your institution is not FDIC-insured. Insured savings associations display the following official logos:

Fig. 1 (FDIC seal and logo)

People in different parts of the country sometimes fall prey to the same pitfalls when making bad deposit insurance decisions. You need to be aware of these problems so you can be on the lookout and avoid them. For instance, a handful of institutions in a few states are insured under state deposit insurance programs and consequently lack FDIC coverage. In many instances, these state insurance programs do not have sufficient funds available to protect consumers adequately. When a state insurance fund is in trouble, the state legislature will normally attempt to cover depositor losses. However, if these losses are significant (and they usually are), the state may have difficulty coughing up enough money to bail out depositors. You may be left in limbo and subjected to lengthy state deliberative processes that ultimately may provide little relief. Given the uncertainties of whether these funds will have sufficient resources to guarantee the safety of your deposits, it is best to avoid state-insured institutions. It is important that you not confuse state-insured with state-chartered institutions. State-insured institutions do not qualify for FDIC coverage; most state-chartered institutions are FDIC-insured.

Some unsuspecting consumers have banked at seemingly reputable businesses that were not financial institutions at all and did not carry any deposit insurance coverage protection of any kind. For example, in Washington, D.C., recently, many customers lost their money when a local institution in which they had faithfully deposited their funds turned out not to be a bank at all. Instead, it was an illegal operation that neither the D.C. government nor the federal government stepped in to correct, despite the fact that it had operated for years. When these kinds of establishments have failed or authorities have shut them down, depositors have often lost everything. Again, look for one of the FDIC logos before handing over your money.

In today's highly competitive financial services marketplace, many providers (insurance agents, stockbrokers, diversified financial services companies, and others) are hawking all sorts of "financial type" products (for example, annuities, life insurance, mutual funds, and stockbrokerage accounts). None of these products is insured. Remember, only banks, savings and loans, and credit unions can offer deposit insurance protection.

If your savings are not FDIC-insured, you should make
every effort to move them into an FDIC-insured institution
as quickly as possible. Checking and savings accounts
should be moved immediately. If you have CDs or other
time deposits at a non-FDIC-insured institution, you are on
the horns of a dilemma. Since moving your money out of a
CD prior to maturity can cost you lost interest and prema-
ture-withdrawal charges, you will probably be better off
keeping your money where it is. In such cases, you need to
monitor very carefully your institution's solvency status.
Keep abreast of the latest developments so you can respond
accordingly, even on short notice. If it becomes apparent
that the institution is in trouble, it may be wise to take a partial loss rather than risk a potential total loss should the institution fail.

❑ Step 2: Shop Around for Sound Financial
        Institutions

The fact that a financial institution is federally insured
does not necessarily mean it is on strong financial footing. It
could still fail. If it is FDIC-insured, however, and you keep
your balances within insured limits (usually up to $100,000),
you should be protected. You may simply have to cope with
the inconvenience of its shutdown by regulators and reopen-
ing under new ownership. To avoid such hassles, you may
want to shop around for an institution that is safe, sound,
and solvent. Just as there is tremendous variation in the
products financial institutionsoffer today, the solvency status of
institutions varies considerably as well. So it is well worth your
while to take some time and do your homework in selecting
a strong financial institution. Moreover, you should periodically reevaluate an institution's status (which can change
quickly), so that you will know if it is on the brink of failure.

Shopping for solvency is not easy. Financial institutions are not required to disclose their solvency ratings. Consequently, while most of their advertisements and promotional materials are chock-full of all sorts of information about their profit-generating products, the solvency status of an institution is usually not included. This information does exist, however, in the form of ratings assigned by the regulators (called CAMEL ratings, short for Capital Assets Management Earnings Liquidity). It would be very helpful if state and federal banking regulators (the people who conduct periodic bank examinations) shared the information they gather. This, however, is closely held, confidential information. Both financial institutions and state and federal banking regulators are prohibited by law from publicly disclosing solvency information.

You may occasionally see a financial institution touting itself as "one of the strongest institutions in the area" or claiming that "our capital levels meet or exceed federal requirements." These pronouncements can be misleading. For example, if all of the institutions in a given area are experiencing problems, being at the top of the heap is not particularly comforting. Similarly, while an institution's capital levels are important, they are not the only criteria that should be considered. If an institution is plagued with problem loans, for example, its existing capital levels, no matter how healthy, could quickly be wiped out.

So how do you get the information you need? For most financial institutions, trouble does not happen overnight. There are usually signs of trouble before a failure results. If an institution is losing money regularly, has delinquent loans outstanding, or has low capital levels, it could be headed for trouble. One way to glean information about your institution's status is to ask your banker. If you ask him or her whether it is safe and sound, you will probably get the pat response: "We are strong." Instead, ask whether your bank earned a profit during the last two calendar quarters. A string of quarterly losses could signal danger. While confronting your bank directly may yield results, you might also ask other banks about your institution's solvency status. With a couple of phone calls to the branch managers of other local institutions, you may be better able to determine how your institution stacks up to others in the area. If everyone you call says your bank is in trouble, it may well be.

Local news stories are often the best sources of information about the conditions of financial institutions. Periodically, articles will appear and stories will air about the solvency status of all financial institutions in a local area. These often take the form of a comparative listing that identifies the strongest and weakest local institutions. Sometimes, after-the-fact stories will chronicle the demise of a particular institution. If your local newspapers, or radio or television stations have not already done solvency stories about financial institutions in your area, encourage them to do so. This would be a tremendous service to the community as well as a great help to you.

Although financial institutions are not allowed to reveal their solvency status per se, they are required to disclose publicly their profit and loss statements on a quarterly basis. These must be published in the local newspaper once a year. They are also often reported on as business news by your local media. Given this, make it a point to scan the business pages of your local newspaper to keep tabs on your financial institution's condition. You might also keep an eye on the interest rates being offered on similar products by different financial institutions in your area. If most of them are paying about 3 percent on their six-month CDs while another institution is offering a substantially higher rate on theirs, this could tip you off that the higher interest rate institution might be experiencing difficulty and desperately trying to attract new business.

You can also get an assessment of your institution's financial condition from a couple of private rating companies. These offer a variety of products and services, including basic information on individual institutions, best and worst listings of local institutions (regional, statewide, county, or city), and detailed, in-depth reports on particular institutions. In some of their reports, these rating services allow you to see your institution's status within a range and understand how it stacks up against other institutions. If you are interested in learning more about the solvency of your institution or of institutions in your area, you might avail yourself of one of these services.

Veribanc and Bauer appear to be the most consumer-friendly of the rating firms, with information presented in easy-to-understand formats. Veribanc uses a color-coded system; Bauer uses a five-star rating system. For the financial sophisticate, other firms are available (for example, Sheshunoff, Weiss Research, Ferguson & Co.) that offer very detailed, highly complex analytical assessments of the solvency status of financial institutions. To order by phone or request an order form, contact:

Veribanc   Bauer Financial Reports
P.O. Box 461   P.O. Drawer 145510
Wakefield, MA 01880-0461   Coral Gables, FL 33114-5510
1-800-442-2657   1-800-388-6686

Veribanc charges $10 for the first rating report and $5 for each additional report. Bauer charges $10 for the first rating report and $2 for each additional report. Both companies accept American Express, MasterCard, and VISA.

Keep in mind, rating services base their analyses and scoring systems on information submitted by institutions in quarterly "call reports" (semiannual reports are required for credit unions). While consumers can get copies of these reports from banking regulators, the information is generally too complex for most of us to understand. Moreover, although the information should be accurate at the time of submission, a particular institution's condition may have improved or deteriorated substantially since the institution turned in its latest report. Given this, neither Veribanc nor Bauer will guarantee the accuracy or completeness of the information they provide. Nonetheless, their information does offer a valuable "snapshot in time" glimpse of where your institution stood when the information was current.

A sticky situation arises if you have term deposits (like a CD) at a financial institution that may be teetering on the brink of insolvency. Should you take your money and run even though you might be subjected to a substantial penalty for early withdrawal and forced to swallow a lower interest rate? If it is a federally insured institution and your balances are within insured amounts, the answer is no. Leave your money where it is; you should be protected. In this situation, it is better to endure the hassles of your institution's takeover than to take radical action and move your account elsewhere. In the future, seek out sound institutions before committing to time deposits.

❑ Step 3:   Keep Your Balances Within Insurance Limits

While most people are aware that deposit insurance covers balances of up to $100,000, some mistakenly believe that this is the maximum insurance for which they can qualify. Depending upon the accounts you have and how they are owned, it is possible to have more than $100,000 in insured deposits at any one institution. Other people mistakenly believe they have more coverage than is actually the case. If you are like most people, you need to understand better the FDIC's rules and make certain your accounts conform to them.

Account Ownership Categories. Deposits maintained in different categories of legal ownership are separately insured. This means that you can have several accounts at the same institution covered up to $100,000 each, just so long as each account falls into a different legal ownership category. Account ownership is generally determined by who is the true owner of funds in an account. The following examples illustrate this point:

Suppose Bob has $100,000 in an <u>individual account</u> at his local bank. Since Bob is the sole owner of funds in the account, he is entitled to $100,000 in insurance protection on it. If Bob's balance goes above $100,000 and his bank fails, he is only entitled to $100,000 in deposit insurance protection.

Bob and his wife, Kate, also have a <u>joint account</u> with a balance of $200,000, which is in both of their names and from which both can access funds. In the event of a bank failure, together they would be entitled to deposit insurance protection of $100,000 for this joint account (in addition to the $100,000 on Bob's individual account). They would <u>not</u> qualify for $100,000 each, despite the total joint account balance of $200,000.

Do not be misled into thinking that you can have numerous accounts in your name at the same institution and each of them will be insured up to $100,000. Deposit insurance coverage is not determined on a "per account" basis. Indeed, the type of account (whether checking, savings, CD, or other deposits) usually has no bearing on the insurance coverage amount. Thus, a person cannot increase insurance coverage merely by dividing deposits owned in the same name into several accounts at the same institution. The balances in these accounts will all be added together to determine deposit insurance coverage.

Similarly, the balances in joint accounts held by the same combination of persons would be totaled and would qualify for only $100,000 in deposit insurance protection. Using the example above:

> *Assume for a moment that Bob and Kate have two joint accounts at the same institution, both with $50,000 balances. The balances in these two accounts would be added together to determine deposit insurance coverage. Since these two account balances yield a grand total of $100,000, these accounts would be fully covered.*

Remember: You can own several different accounts (an individual account plus a joint account with someone else) and qualify for separate deposit insurance coverage on each account as long as each is held in a different name or combination of names. In the above examples, Bob would be entitled to coverage on both his individual account and the joint account he holds with Kate. You can also have more than one insured joint account at an institution, provided each account is owned in a different way and your insurable

interest in all joint accounts at that institution does not exceed $100,000.

Following are some important rules to remember about
joint accounts.

1. Rearranging the names of the owners or changing
   the style of the names does not increase insurance
   coverage.
2. No one joint account can be insured for over
   $100,000.
3. Multiple joint accounts with identical ownership
   cannot be insured for over $100,000 in the aggre-
   gate.
4. No one person's insured interest in all joint accounts at the same institution can exceed $100,000.

Individual and joint accounts are the most common
types of account ownerships. Other types of account ownership that also qualify for separate deposit insurance coverage include testamentary (payable on death) accounts held
for a spouse, child, or grandchild (also called revocable living trust accounts); irrevocable trust accounts; accounts
held in a fiduciary relationship on another's behalf (accounts
held by an agent, conservator, custodian, executor, guard-
ian, or nominee); and business accounts (corporate or partnership, but not sole proprietorship).

Prior to December 19, 1993, you could also qualify for
deposit insurance protection of up to $100,000 on each of
the following: individual retirement accounts (IRAs), self-
directed Keogh plans (retirement plans for self-employed
people), 457 plans (tax-deferred savings plans for employees of state and local governments and nonprofit organizations), and self-directed defined benefit plans (which, in

some instances, could include 401(k) retirement plans). After December 19, 1993, however, you are entitled to only $100,000 for the aggregate of these four types of retirement plans. So if your retirement nest egg accounts at any one institution exceed $100,000, you may need to move some of your retirement savings to another financial institution for it to qualify for deposit insurance protection.

You must also be careful not to change inadvertently the character of your accounts or you could significantly curtail your deposit insurance protection. For example, if you open up an individual account and give someone else the right to withdraw funds from your account (by putting that person's name on a signature card), the account might be insured as a joint account. Similarly, a bank account for a sole proprietorship is viewed as an individual account in your name. Single ownership means accounts held in your own name, those held on your behalf by others, as well as accounts established by a business that is a sole proprietorship.

If you have money in a financial institution and also owe money to the same institution, and the institution fails, you may be able to offset your indebtedness against your deposits for deposit insurance coverage purposes. For example, suppose you have a $150,000 deposit balance and an outstanding loan balance of $50,000. Provided both of these are owned in the same way, you should be able to offset your account balance, including any uninsured portion, against any loans you may have at the bank. Your deposit and indebtedness must, however, both fall into the same ownership categories to qualify for such an offset.

Deposit Insurance Protection at Each Financial Institution in Which You Have Money. Some people mistakenly believe that they are only entitled to up to $100,000 in total deposit insurance protection for accounts they have with different financial institutions. To the contrary, you can qualify for separate deposit insurance protection at any number of institutions. Separate deposit insurance limits apply at each insured institution. So if you have more than $100,000 in an account at one financial institution and want FDIC insurance on the entire balance, you can take the uninsured portion to another FDIC-insured institution and qualify for deposit insurance coverage on accounts you open there.

When you move your money to another financial institution, it must be a distinct, separately chartered institution. If an institution has one or more branches, the main office and all branch offices are considered to be one institution. So if you have deposits in the same ownership category at both the main office and one or more branch offices of the same institution, these similarly held deposits will be added together when calculating deposit insurance coverage.

❑ Step 4: Be on the Lookout for Changes That Might Affect Your Coverage

You also need to be on the lookout for changes that might affect your deposit insurance protection so you can make appropriate adjustments. Some of the common changes of which you should be aware are identified below.

Changes in Your Household and Other Relationships. You should recalculate your insurance coverage after a change in your household, such as when a family member with whom you share a joint account dies. This is because the ownership of certain accounts changes automatically upon death. For example, upon your spouse's death, funds the two of you owned in a joint account would automatically be reclassified as being owned only by you, and would be lumped together with money you may have in an individual account at the same institution. This might very well place you over the $100,000 insurance limit for individual accounts. This could occur upon the death of anyone with whom you share a joint account.

As part of a divorce decree, many couples split joint banking account balances or one spouse may be given sole ownership of a joint account. Again, either of these might throw you over the deposit insurance limit. Similar circumstances can arise if a member of a two-person business partnership dies, leaving the remaining partner with an account in his or her name. So whenever there is a significant change in your household status or other relationships that have banking connotations, it pays to reevaluate your deposit insurance coverage.

Interest Earnings. Keep your balances low enough so that interest payments will not kick them over the $100,000 limit. Once you reach the $100,000 threshold, any additional interest earnings may not be covered by deposit insurance should the institution fail.

Special Life Events. In many of our lives, we experience special events that give us access to sizable sums of money. These include the sale of a home, business, or farm; receipt of insurance proceeds; lump-sum pension distributions; inheritances; gifts; distributions under a trust; proceeds from judicial proceedings. If you are not careful, any of these events can throw the balances in your accounts above deposit insurance limits. Even if these funds are held only temporarily, you probably do not want their addition to force you to exceed deposit insurance levels. Instead, spread your money around in several financial institutions to assure its safety.

When Your Institution's Status Changes. The financial services industry is undergoing a tremendous transformation, with many institutions being acquired by or merging with others. So even if you have money in a couple of different places, should they consolidate into one institution, your accounts will be added together when determining deposit insurance coverage limits. Be careful to take prompt corrective action if this occurs. You should also review your coverage if one of your institutions buys an institution from the FDIC or takes over another troubled institution where you also have money. Be aware of any changes in your institution's status and double-check to make certain you will not be adversely affected.

Changes Mandated by Congress. Still another time to review your deposit insurance coverage is whenever Congress revises deposit insurance rules. For example, the change in retirement account coverage that goes into effect December 19, 1993. When such things happen, you may need to respond. Normally these changes make the news. Your financial institution should notify you about rule changes before they occur, through notices posted in the lobby or mailing inserts included in your statements. Such notifications might also be sent to you in a special mailing. So be on the lookout for notifications of changes that affect your deposits.

❑ **Step 5:   Be Sure the Products You Select Are Insured**
     After you have done all of the above, you must next make certain the products you select are covered by deposit

insurance. Be very careful. Here you cannot rely solely upon the FDIC placard in the lobby. The fact that you are purchasing a product from a financial institution does not necessarily mean that all of the products being sold by the institution are insured. Many institutions today are offering a mixture of insured and uninsured products, all being sold out of the same bank lobby, often by the same people. As a result, it is sometimes very hard to differentiate between what is insured and what is not. Yet, there are tremendous differences between insured and uninsured products. Should your institution fail, your insured deposits will be fully covered up to allowable limits; there is no guarantee that your money in uninsured deposits will be safe.

The resulting confusion is exacerbated by the fact that many institutions are aggressively promoting and trying to steer you toward the uninsured products they offer (because the bank reaps greater profit). On the flip side, the importance and value of many of their insured products (which yield less profit for the bank) tend to be less emphasized. With this in mind, you must be very cautious when shopping for savings and investment products from financial institutions. The following listing will help you identify the types of insured and uninsured products available in many bank lobbies these days.

Insured Deposits
Checking accounts
Savings accounts
NOW accounts
Money market deposit accounts
Christmas Club accounts
Certificates of deposit (CDs)
Trust fund accounts

<u>**Insured Products**</u>

Money orders

Cashier's checks

Officer's checks

Outstanding drafts

Certified checks

Letters of credit (on which the financial institution is primarily liable)

Traveler's checks (on which the financial institution is primarily liable)

<u>**Uninsured Products and Persons**</u>

Annuities

Mutual funds

Insurance products (e.g., life insurance)

Corporate securities (e.g., stocks, bonds)

Government securities (e.g., Treasury bills, bonds, and notes)

Commercial paper (including shares of bank stock)

Creditors of a failed institution

Money market accounts (offered by brokerage firms)

Money market funds

Foreign deposits

If you are not certain whether a particular product is insured, ask the bank representative. But, do not just accept
the bank representative's oral assurances. Ask for written
verification that the product is insured. Keep this evidence
for your records. You might also check around with other
local institutions to see whether they confirm the insurance
status of the product you are considering. Who knows, it
may well be insured and a competitor may offer it or something comparable on more favorable terms. Similarly, confer
with knowledgeable family members and friends whose financial decisions you trust before making a selection you
might later regret. Obviously, there are advantages and dis-

advantages to both insured and uninsured products. The key is to make an informed decision and select the products that are best for you (not for the institution that is selling them).

Should Your Institution Fail

❏ FDIC-insured Institutions

If you have money in an FDIC-insured institution that fails, do not panic. Most people regain access to their insured deposits within a couple of days at the most. If the failed institution is FDIC-insured and your accounts are properly structured, you should be able to recover all of your insured deposits in a fairly short period of time. Even though other people will be clamoring for an immediate response, the best thing for you to do under such circumstances is to be patient and remain calm. Do not rush down to your neighborhood branch with your banking documents in hand prepared to withdraw your money. You may have to tolerate a little inconvenience, but eventually things will get back to normal. This is what deposit insurance is all about.

❏ State-insured Institutions

If you have money in a failed state-insured institution that is not FDIC-insured, state representatives should be on hand at the failed institution advising you of your rights. You will have to look to state banking officials to recoup your money. In such an event, you may wish to contact the State Banking Commission, State Banking Board, or the State Deposit Insurance Fund to get more information about your situation. To protect yourself further, you should probably also write to your elected representatives in the state legislature and to the governor to voice your con-

cerns about getting your money back. All of these people
will probably be located in your state capital.

❑ How Do You Know Your Institution Has Failed?

News travels fast when an institution is taken over by
the FDIC. Normally, there will be a flurry of stories in local
newspapers and on local radio and television stations high-
lighting the failure of the local institution. Or you may hear
about it through word of mouth, see a sudden name change,
witness temporary signs being placed over older bank logos,
or hear bank representatives answer the phone with a different institutional name when you call. You should be aware,
however, that changed names may also mean that your institution has merged with or been taken over by another. In
such cases, a failure has not occurred and the FDIC is not
directly involved.

You are also entitled to formal notification. If a buyer is
found, the assuming institution is required to notify depositors of the failed institution. This is normally accomplished
on the first bank statement mailed to customers after the
changeover has occurred. If no buyer is found, the FDIC is
required to mail you a notification (to your last known address on record at the failed institution) shortly after the failure occurs. Many customers already know about the
institution's demise long before these notices are received.

❑ The Four Basic FDIC Options for Handling Failed Financial Institutions

Purchase and Assumption. A purchase and assumption simply means that the FDIC finds a healthy institution
to purchase the failed institution's assets and assume its deposits (often with financial assistance from the FDIC). Un-

der this approach, both insured and uninsured depositors are fully protected. Hence, no one will lose any money. Since depositors of the failed institution automatically become depositors of the acquiring institution, they should be given quick and easy access to their deposited funds. In some instances, existing accounts are simply transferred to the assuming institution, where customers may be able to write checks and use ATMs just as before their institution closed. You may sometimes be required to open up a new account, order new checks, and get a new ATM card to access your funds. In many instances, customers may be able to transact business as usual on the next business day after the changeover occurs. The only visible difference may be another financial institution's name over the door. Purchase and assumption is the FDIC's most commonly used takeover option.

Insured Deposit Transfer. With an insured deposit transfer, the FDIC will transfer a failed institution's insured deposits (up to $100,000 per account) to a healthy institution in the local area. Under this option, only insured depositors are fully protected. Customers of the failed institution have immediate access to their insured funds at the assuming institution. In most cases, all other assets, including uninsured deposits, will be held and disposed of by the FDIC. The institution that assumes deposits normally does not purchase other assets of the failed institution.

Bridge Bank. If another institution is not available for a purchase and assumption or an insured deposit transfer, the FDIC may organize a special type of bank, called a bridge bank. The FDIC owns and operates a bridge bank, which can provide full banking service to the community for up to five years while a buyer is sought. Only insured depositors are fully protected under the bridge bank approach.

Deposit Payoff. If the FDIC is unable to exercise any of
the above options, it will issue checks to insured depositors
for their account balances up to the $100,000 limit. The
FDIC will normally mail checks to insured depositors within
one to five business days after the failure. You may also be
required to appear at the failed institution to file a claim for
deposit insurance payment or to submit a claim through the
mail. While depositors have up to eighteen months to file
such claims, they should be submitted as soon as possible
after the institution's closing. Only insured deposits are fully
protected under the deposit payoff option. Deposit payoffs
are the FDIC's least-used option.

The FDIC is required by law to use the option that is
least costly to the Bank Insurance Fund and the Savings Association Insurance Fund. Circumstances vary with each
failed institution the FDIC handles.

❑ Status of Uninsured Depositors

As you can see, only through purchase and assumption
are uninsured depositors fully protected by deposit insurance coverage. Under all three of the FDIC's other options,
uninsured depositors are not fully protected. Depositors
over the $100,000 limit may ultimately be covered, but not
immediately. These people might get back some portion of
their uninsured funds, but only after the FDIC sells the
failed institution's assets and recoups its expenses. Recoveries for uninsured depositors may be a long time in coming, if
they occur at all. Even then, uninsured depositors are able
to recoup only a portion of their losses (on a pro rata basis
with all of the bank's other creditors). Recoveries on the uninsured portion of deposits vary from case to case, depend-

ing upon the quality of the failed institution's assets and the FDIC's success in liquidating them. In some limited cases, the FDIC may immediately repay some percentage (but not all) of uninsured deposits if it determines that the failed institution has sufficient assets on hand to cover these obligations. However, uninsured depositors rarely receive immediate and full reimbursement of their funds.

The lesson is obvious: You are playing with fire if you allow your account balances to go beyond the $100,000 maximum. You don't want to be confronted with such distressing circumstances. If you have not yet experienced this and fear you might later fall prey to these problems, by all means get your accounts straightened out immediately. There is absolutely no reason for you to have to grapple with uninsured deposit problems.

❑ Open Bank Assistance

To prevent a financial institution from going under (thereby avoiding the use of one of the four takeover methods above), the FDIC can lend financial assistance to a troubled bank through what is known as open bank assistance. This is rarely used and is available only in the most extraordinary circumstances. For example, open bank assistance may be allowed if the continued operation of the bank is essential to provide services to the local community. Or it might be allowed if local economic conditions are so severe that the bank's failure threatens other financial institutions in the area. Under such circumstances, the bank may be categorized as "too big to fail" and will qualify for open bank assistance. In exchange for this assistance, qualifying financial institutions are required to generate capital from sources other than the FDIC and to demonstrate both that the institution is not engaged in unsound banking practices

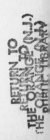

and that it can be restored to health. Under open bank assistance, the institution does not fail and its assets are not taken over by the FDIC. Thus, all of the institution's depositors are fully protected.

❏ What Are Your Options If Your Institution Fails?

After access to your money has been restored and your financial institution reopens (albeit under a different name), you may wish to leave your money where it is. The likelihood that your institution will experience another deposit insurance crisis at any point in the near future is small. Once the FDIC has intervened, your deposits should be on stable ground.

If you have CDs or other savings at a now failed bank, these can be revised, rescinded, or sold. It is possible for a long-term CD (or any other existing deposits) on which you are currently earning 8 percent to be voided by the acquiring institution. You do not lose your money, however. You may or may not be able to keep your CD at the same rate if your institution is taken over. If not, high-rate CDs will probably be canceled by the acquiring institution. You will then be given the opportunity either to accept a new CD at a lower interest rate or to move your money to another institution (within a limited time span). The rates at other institutions, however, will probably be close to what the acquiring institution is willing to offer.

If you have an outstanding loan or other indebtedness with an institution that has been taken over by the FDIC, you are still required to make your scheduled payments. Even though this debt may be owned by someone new (an acquiring bank or the FDIC), your obligation to pay does not change. Similarly, if you have direct deposits, automatic bill payments, and other similar features, these will follow your accounts to the acquiring institution.

Deposit Insurance Problems and Assistance

If you have any questions, desire further information, have a deposit insurance problem, or wish to register a complaint about deposit insurance coverage, for federally insured banks and savings and loan associations, contact:

Federal Deposit Insurance Corporation
Office of Consumer Affairs
550 17th St., NW
Washington, DC 20429
1-800-934-3342

The toll-free consumer inquiry "hot line" allows you to access computerized tapes on various deposit insurance issues around the clock. Personalized assistance is available during office hours, 9 A.M.-5 P.M. EST.
For problems or questions with federally insured credit unions, contact:

National Credit Union Administration
1776 G St., NW
Washington, DC 20456

Since deposit insurance is a federal issue of concern to the United States Congress, you might wish to share your views with or seek assistance from your two U.S. senators and your member of the U.S. House of Representatives. Both senators and representatives can be reached through the Capitol switchboard at (202) 224-3121. Correspondence should be mailed to the following addresses:

The Honorable_____
United States Senate
Washington, DC 20510

The Honorable_____
United States House of Representatives
Washington, DC 20515

R E C O M M E N D A T I O N S

Remember, to protect yourself against deposit insurance problems you need to take the following steps.

Step 1: Put your money in federally insured institutions only.

Step 2: Shop around for sound institutions.

Step 3: Keep your balances within insurance limits.

Step 4: Be on the lookout for changes that might affect your coverage.

Step 5: Be sure the products you select are insured.

Should an institution in which you have money fail, do not panic. While you may be subjected to some uncertainty and inconvenience, your deposited funds will be protected if you have followed the above steps. The FDIC has a number of options available to resolve deposit insurance problems. Your best bet is to make absolutely certain all of your money is in insured deposits at qualifying institutions. If you have problems or complaints about deposit insurance issues, contact the FDIC.

NOTES

2

Checking and NOW Accounts

Jill and Joan both have checking accounts with fluctuating balances that average $1000. But each year, Jill earns $40 in interest and pays no fees while Joan earns no interest and pays $200 in fees.

With the exception of payment by cash, writing checks is the most frequent way that consumers make payments. Nearly 80 percent of households maintain some type of checking account, and the typical household writes about twenty checks per month. A large majority of these accounts are with full-service banking institutions—commercial banks, S&Ls, or credit unions.

In the 1980s, checking accounts changed in several important respects. First, in 1980 the federal government permitted credit unions to issue share drafts that pay interest,

and in early 1981 it allowed banks and savings and loans to
pay interest on the money in checking accounts. These accounts are called Negotiable Order of Withdrawal (NOW)
accounts.

Second, partly to make up the interest paid to customers
on NOW accounts, banking institutions substantially increased their fees for writing, depositing, bouncing, and
stopping payment on checks. In the early 1980s, total fees
charged by banks on all checking and savings accounts rose
from $5 billion to $10 billion. Since then, these fees have
continued to escalate. On typical accounts, when minimums
are not met, banks are now charging monthly service fees as
high as $10 for a regular checking account and $15 for a
NOW account. Moreover, some charge as much as $.50 to
write a check, $1 to use an automated teller machine
(ATM), $25 for a bounced check, $25 to stop payment on a
check, and $26 to purchase 150 checks.

Checking Options

There are four basic types of checking accounts. Two of
these—NOW accounts and share drafts—earn interest, and
two do not. The two types of non-interest-earning accounts
are called by various names. But usually one type waives
monthly and per-check service fees if a minimum or average
balance requirement is maintained. This "regular checking"
is offered by most banks and savings and loans. The other
type has no minimum balance requirement yet charges
monthly and per-check fees. These fee-only accounts, however, are offered by only about one-third of institutions.
("Lifeline" checking accounts with no or very low regular

service charges and no minimum balance requirements are offered by a small minority of banks.)

Most banks and savings and loans offer all types of accounts except share drafts, which are issued only by credit unions. The table below summarizes the typical features of these four accounts. Although the fees in the table are typical, they are not the same at all institutions. In fact, the monthly minimum to avoid fees on regular checking tends to be much higher than the no-fee minimum on certain NOW accounts. In some cases, the monthly fee on regular checking is higher than the fee charged on NOW accounts. Also, many banking institutions offer free checking to older customers.

TYPICAL FEATURES OF CHECKING ACCOUNTS

Type of Account	Interest Rate	Minimum to Avoid Fees	Mo. Service Charge	Per-Check Charge
Fee-only	None	None	$4.00	$.25
Regular	None	$400	$5.00	$.20*
NOW	2.5%	$1,000	$7.50	$.20*
Share draft	3.0%	$150**	$2.00	$.15*

*Assessed when balance drops below the required minimum.
**Most credit unions have no minimum balance requirement.

If you cannot maintain the minimum balance in a regular account, you should select a fee-only account. If you write only a few checks, you will find that the monthly charges are usually lower. But if you can maintain the minimum, it is preferable to have a regular account, since no service charges or transaction fees will be assessed. Only those who can meet minimum balance requirements should maintain NOW accounts. When these requirements are not met, monthly fees almost always far exceed interest earned.

❑ Fee-only Checking

Fee-only checking is offered by about one-third of all banks and savings and loans. These accounts are advertised for infrequent check writers with low balances. No interest is paid on these accounts. The fees are often advertised as lower than those on regular checking and NOW accounts. Fees on these accounts, however, are not significantly lower than those on regular checking, except on lifeline accounts. Created for small depositors with low incomes, lifeline accounts typically charge no or very low fees, but limit the number of transactions (most commonly between five and ten a month). They are offered by only a few institutions, which sometimes tie them to ATM use.

Fees. On most no-minimum accounts, typically there is a monthly service fee and/or charge for each check written. When only one or the other fee is charged, the fees are higher. For example, a typical fee is $4 a month for service and $.25 for each check written. If there is only a monthly fee, it is likely to be $5. If there is only a per-check charge, it is likely to be $.30 to $.35. Some institutions also charge fees for deposits (individual checks and/or deposit slips) and ATM transactions.

Cost to Consumers. The cost of maintaining a no-minimum checking account varies with both the institution and the level of activity. The following table indicates the annual cost of a fee-only account with a $4 monthly service charge and $.25 per-check charges for different levels of activity.

As the following table reveals, the costs of fee-only accounts are not low. They emphasize the desirability of finding a regular checking account with an affordable minimum balance to avoid monthly and per-check charges.

ANNUAL COSTS OF FEE-ONLY CHECKING

Level of Activity	Cost
5 checks/mo.	$ 63
10 checks/mo.	$ 78
20 checks/mo.	$108
30 checks/mo.	$138

❑ **Regular Checking**

Regular checking is offered by most banks and savings and loans. Unlike fee-only accounts, on regular checking accounts monthly service and transaction fees are not assessed when a minimum (or average) balance is maintained. When this balance is not kept, nearly all institutions charge a monthly service fee and most assess per-check fees as well.

Minimums to Avoid Fees. The minimum balance required to avoid charges on a regular checking account varies greatly, ranging from $100 to several thousand dollars. Even though the median balance is $400, in most areas the required minimum balance ranges widely. For example, according to a Consumer Action 1992 survey of California banking institutions, minimum balances to avoid fees range from $100 to $2,500, with most running between $500 and $750. In the Washington, D.C., area, minimums range from $100 to $4,000.

Some banks provide consumers the option of maintaining an average monthly balance, which is usually higher than the minimum. If your checking balance fluctuates greatly, this option can save you money. There is a tremendous range in the amount required for an average balance account. But at $1,000, the typical average is significantly higher than the typical minimum.

Fees. When minimum or average balances are not maintained, fees are assessed. Almost all banks charge a monthly service fee that may vary depending on how low the balance drops—the lower the balance, the higher the fee. Many also charge a fee for each check written. Monthly service and per-check fees at these banks are usually lower than those at institutions without per-check charges. A number of institutions with per-check fees also charge for deposits and/or ATM transactions.

Monthly service fees and per-check charges vary greatly among banking institutions, even within the same area. In the Consumer Action survey, for instance, monthly fees at those institutions assessing them ranged from $2 to $12. Moreover, at several of these institutions assessing per-check charges, there is a fee of $.50 per check.

These checking fees tend to be highest at New York City-based money center banks, where, for example, Citibank, Chase Manhattan, and Chemical charge a $9.50 monthly service fee and per-check fees ranging from $.25 to $.35. In the Washington, D.C., area, Citibank charges a $10 monthly fee and $.25 per-check fee.

Cost to Consumers. The annual cost of maintaining a regular checking account when the minimum balance requirement is not met varies considerably, as the table below shows.

Particularly for moderate and frequent check writers, it is important to maintain the minimum or average balance necessary to avoid fees. If this is impossible, moderate and frequent check writers should select an account with a low monthly service charge but no transaction fees.

ANNUAL COSTS OF REGULAR CHECKING*

Charges	Number of Checks Written Per Month		
	10	20	30
$5 mo. fee/no per-check fee	$ 60	$ 60	$ 60
$10 mo. fee/no per-check fee	$120	$120	$120
$5 mo. fee/$.25 per-check fee	$ 90	$120	$150
$10 mo. fee/$.25 per-check fee	$150	$180	$210

*When minimum or average balance requirements are not met.

❏ NOW Accounts

NOW accounts are offered by almost all banks and savings and loans. When minimum (or average) balances are kept, interest is earned. When different and usually higher minimum or average balances are maintained, there are usually no monthly service and transaction fees. NOW account minimums are usually higher than those on regular checking. When the minimums are not met, the fees are also generally higher.

Interest Minimums and Rates. At most banks and savings and loans, either no minimum balance must be maintained to earn interest or the minimum is fairly low ($200 or less). Yet, there are notable exceptions. For example, at three California institutions surveyed by Consumer Action—California State Bank, Coast Federal Bank, and Ventura County Bank—minimum balances of at least $2,500 must be kept, and these fees usually exceed interest earned.

In early 1993, the typical institution paid less than 3 percent on NOW accounts. Some banks, including Citibank and Chemical in New York City, paid a rate under 2 percent.

Most institutions compound interest daily. But a number compound only monthly, and a few compound quarterly (every three months). The most favorable method of compounding is continuous on a 365/360-day basis. (While most banks operate on a 360-day year, some pay interest on all 365 days.) But unless huge balances are involved, the difference between continuous and daily compounding is not significant—less than one-tenth of one percentage point in interest earned. On the other hand, continuous compounding pays an interest rate four-tenths of a percentage point higher than does quarterly compounding. Given the option, you should avoid quarterly compounded accounts.

Minimums to Avoid Fees. At almost all banks and savings and loans, minimum (or average) balances must be maintained to avoid monthly service and transaction fees on NOW accounts. These minimums range from $100 to $10,000. Most institutions have a minimum between $500 and $1,500, with $1,000 most common.

Some institutions allow either a minimum or an average balance to be maintained to avoid fees. Typically the average balance requirement is double the minimum balance requirement. If balances fall to several hundred dollars, it may be easier to avoid fees by maintaining the average than the minimum balance.

To allow you to avoid regular fees, some institutions offer the option of keeping an average balance in either an individual retirement account (IRA) or a minimum balance in a savings account held at the same bank. These average balances can range from $1,000 to $5,000, with most between $2,000 and $3,000.

Fees. When minimum balances are not maintained, monthly service and/or transaction fees are charged. At most institutions these fees are either the same as or somewhat higher than fees on regular checking; they are never lower. Also, monthly service fees tend to be highest at those banks and savings and loans without transaction charges.

Monthly service fees vary widely, not only throughout the nation but even within one region. In the Washington, D.C., area, for example, they can range from $5 to $15. In California, according to the Consumer Action survey, they range from $3.50 to $12.

As they do for regular checking, several New York City—based money center banks charge high fees on NOW accounts. Citibank charges $15 in Washington, D.C., and $12 in New York City, while Chase Manhattan and Chemical both charge $12. There are many other areas, however, where institutions which charge monthly service fees as high as $12.

A number of banking institutions charge a fee for each check written in addition to a monthly service fee. These per-check fees typically range from $.20 to $.50 at different institutions. In general, at any one institution with a per-check fee, the higher this fee, the lower the monthly service charge. But again, New York City-based money center banks are the exception; in New York City, for example, they assess $.35 per-check charges as well as $12 monthly service fees when minimum balance requirements are not met.

Cost to Consumers. The annual cost of a NOW account when the minimum balance requirement is not maintained varies considerably. When monthly service and per-check fees are assessed, consumers usually must pay more than $100 annually. For frequent check writers at several money center banks, annual charges may well exceed $200.

ANNUAL COSTS OF NOW ACCOUNTS*

Charges	Number of Checks Written Per Month		
	10	20	30
$7 monthly fee/no per-check fee	$ 84	$ 84	$ 84
$12 monthly fee/no per-check fee	$144	$144	$144
$7 monthly fee/$.25 per check fee	$114	$144	$174
$12 monthly fee/$.35 per check fee	$186	$228	$270

*When minimum or average balance requirements are not met.

These costs illustrate the importance, especially to frequent check writers, of meeting minimum or average balance requirements. If this is not possible, choose a regular checking account with a low monthly service fee and no transaction charges.

❑ **Share Drafts**

Interest-bearing checking accounts called share drafts are offered by about 80 percent of all credit unions. They are the credit union equivalent of NOW accounts offered by banks and savings and loans.

Most credit unions offering these accounts impose no routine charges, regardless of the size of the account. Among the few that do charge, fees can often be avoided by keeping a relatively low minimum balance in the account—about $150 for the largest credit unions and about $350 for the smallest ones. Credit unions that charge when the account is below the minimum impose average fees of $2 per month and/or per-check fees that average around 15 cents per check.

The average interest rate on share drafts is slightly higher—often several tenths of a percentage point—than that paid by banks and savings and loans on NOW accounts.

Special Charges and Limits

Check Purchases. Most banks and savings and loans offer several types of checks. The cost depends on whether the checks are personalized or printed on fancy paper, and varies from institution to institution. For instance, two hundred of the least expensive checks cost between $5 and $18 at a couple dozen institutions in four different cities. For a very frequent check writer of four hundred checks per year at a cost of $10 to $36, the range of costs then would be $26. But since most consumers write far fewer checks, and since most institutions charge $8 to $12 for two hundred checks, this expense should not be a major factor in choosing an account.

Check Holds. Banks and savings and loans "hold" some deposited checks for a period of time before releasing the funds to you. These holding periods typically grow longer as the distance increases between the bank on which the check was written and the bank where the check was deposited. A check drawn on a California institution deposited in a New York account would be subjected to the longest holding periods.

A relatively new federal law mandates that, except under certain conditions, check holds can be no longer than two days on checks written on banks in the same area and five days on checks written on institutions outside the state. Moreover, some institutions are willing to make deposited funds immediately available, especially if there are funds of an equivalent amount in a savings account. Consumers who do not keep large balances in their checking account and worry about bouncing checks should look for institutions that do not hold checks.

The check hold limits do not apply, however, when you deposit, in one day, checks totaling more than $5,000; when you deposit a check that has been returned unpaid; when you have frequently overdrawn your account in recent months; or when the bank has reason to believe that your check will not be paid—for example, if you have submitted other checks from the same payer that were not paid.

Bouncing several checks a year can be costly at most banking institutions, since the typical charge is $15, according to a recent Federal Reserve survey. But this charge varies from institution to institution—from $10 to $20 in the Consumer Action survey of California institutions, and from $9.50 to $25 in our four-city survey. Accordingly, at some institutions, bouncing four or five checks a year can cost as much as $100 or more.

Stop Payments. Stopping payment on a check is almost as expensive as bouncing a check. The Federal Reserve survey found that a typical charge was $12. But our four-city survey revealed a range of charges from $10 to $25. Thus, stopping payment on four checks a year can cost as much as $100.

Canceled-Check Truncation. Most consumers value the return of their canceled checks. These provide a far more complete and valuable record of payments than do monthly statements. For some transactions, a canceled check is a consumer's only proof of purchase.

In spite of this, banking institutions have been trying to truncate this service—retain the canceled checks themselves and provide consumers with only a monthly statement listing check numbers and amounts. Truncation allows banks to avoid the time and expense of mailing canceled checks back to their customers.

A few banks simply impose truncation, allowing no other option. Many others offer incentives to encourage truncation, such as lower fees or the payment of interest on account balances.

Many institutions with truncated accounts will make copies of checks available for free, but some charge a fee. Our survey revealed that this fee can be as much as $5 per check.

Inquiries. Increasingly, banks and savings and loans charge fees for providing information about personal accounts. A majority, for example, now charge a fee for responding to a phone inquiry about your checking balance. The fee for one inquiry is typically $1 but can be as high as $2. An increasing number charge for a record of an ATM transaction.

Inactive Accounts and Early Closure. Some banks and savings and loans charge consumers for accounts that are inactive or closed within a year of opening. One bank, for example, charges a monthly fee of $2 on accounts under $500 with no transactions in the previous six months. It continues to assess the fee until a check is written, a deposit is made, or the customer notifies the bank that he or she is aware the account exists.

Less reasonable is the practice of charging a fee for closing an account within a year after it is opened. One institution, for instance, charges $25 for terminating an account within the first year. Since you may wish to close an account early if your bank substantially hikes its charges, you should avoid banks that charge closure fees.

Miscellaneous Services

❑ Overdraft Protection

Many banks and savings and loans offer a credit line that becomes an automatic loan if you write a check for more than your account balance. These loan programs are variously called credit lines, no-bounce checking, overdraft privileges, cash advance, and advance accounts. They are similar to one another in that they lend you funds to cover overdrafts. A credit line can help you avoid bounced-check fees.

Institutions lend either the exact amount of the overdraft or an amount in a multiple of $100, $500, or $1,000. The annual percentage rate (APR) charged on these loans approximates the rate charged on unpaid credit card purchases—roughly 18 to 22 percent. In addition, some institutions assess a monthly service fee or a per-loan fee when overdrafts are covered.

The method of repayment varies considerably. Some institutions automatically repay the loan or loans with deposited funds, either the day of the deposit or at the end of the billing period. Other institutions require you to make formal payment, usually after receiving monthly statements. Many make a predetermined automatic payment from funds in the account on the statement date.

Generally, the smaller the credit line, the easier it is to obtain. Some institutions require you to fill out an extensive credit application; others will extend this protection to you if you are a long-term customer who has demonstrated an ability to manage your account. At some institutions, a credit line is a feature of a bank card that is available only to the bank's credit card customers.

In addition to a credit line, some institutions allow overdrafts to be covered by a savings account. Typically there is a service charge for each of these overdrafts of up to $1.

❑ Safe-Deposit Boxes

Safe-deposit boxes are useful for keeping jewelry and valuable papers, including securities, insurance policies, and proof of insured valuables. Unfortunately, the price of renting safe-deposit boxes has risen significantly over the past decade. In the Federal Reserve survey, the annual rental averaged $16.95. This rental had risen from less than $10 a decade ago, and the annual rental was as high as $40 at one institution. Some institutions, however, will waive the fee entirely if substantial deposits are maintained.

❑ Money Orders, Cashier's Checks, and Certified Checks

Consumers without a checking account may wish to pay bills and make other fund transfers with money orders. Fifteen years ago, most of these payments cost less than $.50. Today, according to the Federal Reserve survey, the typical money order costs $2.00. At this price, writing five money orders a month would cost $120 a year. This expense is considerably more than that of writing checks on an account in which the minimum balance to avoid fees is maintained.

Some banking institutions sell money orders only to depositors. Others assess regular customers a lower fee. One bank, for example, charges depositors $2.00 and non-depositors $4.00.

Banks and savings and loans sell cashier's checks as an alternative to money orders. Although both serve the same purpose, institutions limit the size of money orders, but not the size of cashier's checks. Typically, they charge the same price for a money order and a cashier's check of the same amount. But they assess a high fee for cashier's checks written for large amounts.

Another, more expensive alternative to money orders is a certified check. At many institutions, the cost of this check is two to four times the cost of money orders and cashier's checks.

❏ Check Cashing

Most banks and savings and loans cash the checks of depositors only. They do not even cash the Social Security and welfare checks of noncustomers. Institutions that are willing to do so typically assess high fees, usually more than $5. Legislation to require banking institutions to cash government checks for reasonable fees is being considered by Congress and in many state legislatures across the country.

C H E C K L I S T

Use this checklist when shopping for checking or NOW accounts.

For NOW Accounts:
    Interest rate
    Method of compounding   _____
    Minimum (average) balance to earn interest   _____

For NOW and Checking Accounts:
    Minimum balance to avoid regular fee   _____
    Regular fees
    ○ Monthly service   _____
    ○ Per check written   _____
    ○ Per deposit   _____
    ○ Per ATM transaction   _____

    Special fees
    ○ Bounced check
    ○ Stop payment   _____
    ○ Returned deposits   _____
    ○ Purchasing checks   _____
    ○ Balance inquiries   _____
    ○ Early closure   _____

    Other features
    ○ Interest paid during hold period?
    ○ Required truncation   _____
    ○ Credit line, amount and cost   _____

R E C O M M E N D A T I O N S

The most important way to keep checking costs low is to meet minimum (or average) balance requirements so that monthly service and per-check fees are not assessed. If these fees are charged, they may exceed $200 a year.

Minimum balance requirements vary greatly from bank to bank and from account to account. Select an institution with a balance requirement that you can meet every month.

Although balance requirements tend to be higher on NOW accounts than on regular checking accounts, NOW accounts pay interest. But keep in mind that a 3 percent interest rate on a $2,000 average balance will yield only $60 in interest during a year. Also remember that other savings vehicles such as certificates of deposit (CDs) and even U.S. savings bonds usually pay higher yields than do NOW accounts. So it is usually unwise to keep large sums in a NOW account. While the size of this amount will vary from depositor to depositor, most consumers are not wise to keep more than $10,000 in a NOW account.

In selecting a checking account, also consider the number and size of special fees for bounced checks, stop payments, purchasing checks, and balance inquiries. If you frequently pay these fees, find an institution where they are low.

3

Savings Options:
An Overview

Jim and John each had $20,000 in savings. But Jim earned only $500 in interest on his money in a pass-book savings account while John earned $1,100 on his deposit in a five-year certificate of deposit.

How to Evaluate Savings Options

The three fundamental factors you should consider in evaluating savings options are risk, liquidity, and yield. These factors are interdependent. There is no savings vehicle that offers low risk, high liquidity, and high yield. You must weigh the importance of each and make compromises.

Risk. Risk is the possibility of receiving a lower yield than expected on an investment, or even losing part or all of your principal. The market rewards investors for bearing two basic types of risk. The first is risk of default: the possibility that the financial institution will be unable to make timely payments of interest or principal. You can avoid risk of default by putting your savings in accounts insured by the federal government or by purchasing securities issued by the federal government. Accounts at institutions insured by private insurance funds are not free from this risk.

The second type of risk is market risk: the possibility that the market value of your investment will decline because interest rates have increased. Market risk is a factor only in savings or investments that pay a fixed interest rate, such as fixed-rate CDs or savings bonds, and it depends on the length of time to maturity—the longer away the maturity date of a financial instrument, the greater its market risk. For savings, this is because the longer away the maturity date, the longer the time during which interest rates can rise. Variable-rate savings options, such as variable-rate CDs and money market accounts, have no market risk because their rates change with the market.

Liquidity. Liquidity measures the ease and cost of converting your investment into cash. The most liquid assets are cash and checking accounts, which are payable on demand. Savings accounts are slightly less liquid than checking accounts because the issuing institution can make account holders wait for their money. Somewhat less liquid than savings accounts are securities traded on the open market, such as Treasury bills. The least liquid assets are real estate, precious gems, and collectibles. Although they are not negotiable, CDs issued by commercial banks, savings and loans, and credit unions are somewhat liquid because most issuers are willing to redeem them for cash before they mature (albeit at a cost to the owner). Only assets that are reasonably liquid are appropriate for use as savings vehicles.

Yield. Yield is the rate of return on your investment on an annual basis. Factors affecting yield include the interest rate paid, the method used to compute the interest earned, and the frequency with which that interest is compounded. In general, the more liquid a savings option, the lower its yield. Also, the greater the risk of a savings vehicle, the greater the yield. Riskier assets also tend to be less liquid than those with lower risk.

In addition to risk, liquidity, and yield, the following factors influence the desirability of a particular savings option.

Transaction Costs. You may incur charges when buying or selling a financial instrument. These charges can be substantial. For example, Treasury security transactions of under $100,000 are subject to a flat fee. Some banks and brokerage houses charge $50 or more for buying or selling a Treasury bill. Some have recently started imposing a fee for cashing the coupons attached to Treasury securities, which represent the interest they pay. You can substantially reduce these costs by shopping around for brokerage services or by buying Treasury securities directly from the Federal Reserve.

Institutional Fees. Banks and savings and loans often charge a variety of fees for savings accounts, most commonly for inactive accounts and for accounts closed shortly after they are opened. Some institutions charge savers as much as $5 a month to maintain accounts in which there has

been no activity for ninety days. Others charge fees for savings account withdrawals in excess of three per month, or
for ATM deposits or withdrawals.

Negotiability. You can sell negotiable savings instruments to a third party. You cannot sell nonnegotiable instruments on the open market, but you can exchange them for
cash at the issuing institution. All savings accounts and all
CDs under $100,000 are nonnegotiable. Money market
funds are negotiable. Treasury securities are negotiable, but
U.S. savings bonds are not.

Expandability. In general, once you purchase a bond or
CD, you cannot add to the principal, and may not even be
able to reinvest the interest you earn. On the other hand,
you can add to money market funds and money market accounts, but some accounts restrict additions (other than the
reinvestment of interest) to amounts of $100 or more.

Convenience. The convenience with which you can
purchase a security or open and maintain an account varies
among different savings vehicles and among different financial institutions offering the same vehicles. For example,
some financial institutions will automatically deduct a set
sum from your checking account and transfer it to your
money market savings account each month. Others will not.

Minimum Investment. The minimum amount of money
you need to purchase a savings vehicle varies widely. Some
savings options require $5,000 or more, whereas many insti-
tutions will open a passbook savings account with an initial
deposit of only $10.

Other Services. Many banks and some brokerage
houses offer you a variety of free or low-cost services if you
meet certain initial investment requirements. Some of these
services can be valuable, such as free check printing. Others
are nothing more than "bells and whistles," such as discounts on merchandise that is often available for the same
price or less at discount stores.

❑ **Six Ways to Save**
Regular Savings Accounts. Regular savings accounts
are offered by credit unions, commercial banks, and savings
and loans. They require very small initial deposits, and they
can be added to or withdrawn from in any amount at any
time and consequently are almost as liquid as cash.

The basic disadvantage of regular savings accounts is
that they pay relatively low yields. Moreover, many banks
impose a variety of charges against these accounts, which
under certain circumstances can exceed the interest earned.

Regular savings accounts are usually the least attractive
option for savers that can keep at least $1,000 on account.
But these accounts may be a reasonable option for small
savers, if the banking institution does not charge fees for
low balances. At almost all banking institutions, regular savings accounts are insured by the federal government up to
$100,000 per depositor.

Money Market Accounts (MMAs). Money market accounts are offered by credit unions, banks, and savings and
loans. Usually they require larger initial deposits to open the
account and larger minimum balances to avoid fees than do
regular savings accounts. But they pay a slightly higher interest rate and give depositors the opportunity to write up

to three checks per month on the account.

Money market accounts should only be considered by those who can meet minimum balance requirements to avoid fees. If minimums are not met and average balances are not large, savers pay more in fees than the interest they earn.

At almost all banking institutions, money market accounts are insured by the federal government up to $100,000 per account.

Money Market Funds (MMFs). Money market funds are offered by firms regulated by the Securities and Exchange Commission (SEC). They invest in short-term financial instruments such as Treasury bills, commercial paper (short-term unsecured obligations of major corporations), negotiable CDs issued by commercial banks, and banker's acceptances (a type of negotiable postdated check that is guaranteed by a major commercial bank). The yield of these funds changes daily, reflecting fluctuations in market conditions. Usually these accounts pay you slightly higher yields than those of money market accounts.

Most money market funds require an initial deposit of $1,000 to open an account, but after that, allow your balance to fall below that amount. The account can be added to or drawn from at any time, although transactions are generally limited to a minimum of $100. Some funds allow you to write checks against your balance.

The major limitation of MMFs is that they are not insured by the federal government. Investors in such funds, however, should be aware that, mainly because of the funds' conservative investment strategies, the risk of default is very slight. No investor in a money market fund has, to date, lost the funds he or she deposited.

Certificates of Deposit (CDs). CDs are offered by
credit unions, banks, and savings and loans. In almost all areas, these accounts are available to savers with as little as
$500, and they pay a yield that is almost always higher than
that on regular savings accounts, money market accounts,
and money market funds. In general, the larger the amount
deposited, the higher the yield.

The trade-off is that you must leave your money on deposit for a certain period of time or incur a penalty. The
longer the period of time, the higher the yield.

At almost all banking institutions, CDs are insured by
the federal government up to $100,000 per depositor.

U.S. Savings Bonds. U.S. savings bonds are issued by
the federal government and are sold by most credit unions,
banks, and savings and loans. The series EE bonds are those
that combine the greatest availability and highest yields.

Like a CD, the longer these bonds are held, the higher
the yield. In January 1993, if you held a EE bond for at least
five years, you were guaranteed a minimum rate of 6 percent. A bond held only six months yielded more than 4 percent. Thus, at present EE bonds usually offer higher yields
than do savings accounts, money market accounts, money
market funds, and even CDs.

Savings bonds offer several other attractive features.
They can be purchased in denominations as small as $75.
Second, taxes on their earnings are not payable until the
bonds are cashed. Funds deposited in U.S. savings bonds
are guaranteed by the federal government up to any amount.
The principal limitation of these bonds is lack of liquidity.
There is a severe penalty for withdrawing funds before the
bond matures.

Short-Term Treasury Securities. The U.S. Treasury fi-
nances our $4-trillion national debt by selling securities on
the open market at competitively determined interest rates.
You can purchase Treasury securities directly through a
Federal Reserve Bank or with the aid of a broker or bank.
These securities are safe and liquid. Long-term Treasuries
do carry a considerable amount of market risk, which increases with years to maturity (as is the case with all debt
securities).

Treasury securities are exempt from all state and local
taxes except estate taxes. This can be of considerable benefit to you if you live in a high-tax state.

The Treasury issues three types of securities: bills,
notes, and bonds. Bills are issued with maturities of fifty-
two weeks or less, in minimum denominations of $10,000,
with $5,000 increments thereafter. Notes have maturities of
one to ten years. The smallest note available with a maturity
of less than four years is usually $4,000. Notes with
maturities of four years or more can be purchased in denominations of $1,000. Bonds have maturities of ten to
thirty years, and are issued in minimum denominations of
$1,000.

It is easiest to purchase a Treasury bill from a bank or
broker, but if you wish to purchase it directly from the Federal Reserve, you must submit a tender (which is nothing
more than a special form) to the Federal Reserve or one of
its branches no later than 1:30 P.M., Eastern time the day of
the auction. If you mail the form, you should send it directly
to the Treasury. You should indicate on the tender that you
are submitting a noncompetitive bid, and whether or not
you want to have the funds reinvested when the bill matures. Payment must accompany the tender.

Since Treasury bills are issued at a discount from face value, you will have to send more than the cost of the bill with your tender. A refund check for the difference between the price of the bill and your payment will be sent to you shortly after the auction.

The procedure for purchasing Treasury notes and bonds is similar to the procedure for purchasing bills, but has some differences. You can pay with a personal check. And there is no automatic reinvestment option.

Because the direct purchase of Treasury notes, bills, and bonds is relatively complicated, you should consider contacting the nearest Federal Reserve Bank for advice. These banks are located in Atlanta, Baltimore, Birmingham, Boston, Buffalo, Charlotte, Chicago, Cincinnati, Cleveland, Dallas, Denver, Detroit, El Paso, Houston, Jacksonville, Kansas City, Little Rock, Los Angeles, Louisville, Memphis, Miami, Minneapolis, Nashville, New Orleans, New York, Oklahoma City, Omaha, Philadelphia, Pittsburgh, Portland, Richmond, Salt Lake City, San Antonio, San Francisco, Seattle, and St. Louis.

❑ Comparing the Six Options: A Summary

By showing the most important features of various savings accounts, the following table compares these six options.

Keep in mind, however, that interest rates vary over time for all of these savings options except for U.S. Series EE savings bonds. By the end of 1993 or 1994, yields on these bonds may not compare as favorably with those on other options as they did in January 1993.

SAVINGS OPTIONS (JANUARY 1993)

Account	Approximate Average Rate*	Access Restricted	Federally Guaranteed**
Regular savings	2.5%	No	Yes
Money market account	2.7%	No	Yes
Money market fund	2.8%	No	No
CD-6 month	3.0%	Yes	Yes
CD-5 year	5.5%	Yes	Yes
U.S. EE savings bond-6 months	4.2%	Yes	Yes
U.S. EE savings bond-5 years	6.0%	Yes	Yes
Treasury-3 month	3.2%	Yes	Yes
Treasury-5 year	5.6%	Yes	Yes

*Rates as of January 1993. Assumes minimum balance requirements to earn interest and
 avoid fees are met.
**Almost all credit unions, banks, and savings and loans offering these accounts are federally
 insured.

R E C O M M E N D A T I O N S

To allow for unexpected expenses, all consumers should have savings in a low-risk or risk-free account. Single persons and two-income couples should keep at least three months' income, and families should keep at least six months' income, in savings.

The most important factors to consider in evaluating savings options are yield, risk, and liquidity. Money market accounts, money market funds, CDs, Treasury securities, and savings bonds are the savings options that should be considered most seriously.

NOTES

4

Regular Savings Accounts

Gail and Gladys both kept $900 in a regular savings account at different banks. Gail earned $36 in interest each year and paid no fees. Unfortunately, because of a high minimum balance requirement to avoid fees, the $24 that Gladys earned in interest each year was more than offset by $60 in fees.

If you wish to save regularly but have only modest amounts of money to put aside, you should consider regular savings accounts. There are two types: passbook accounts and statement savings accounts. The principal difference between them is that with the former, your record is a passbook; with the latter, it is a monthly statement. Since banks are trying to phase out passbooks, some offer more favorable terms for statement accounts.

Before congressional passage of Truth-in-Savings legislation in late 1991, yields on savings accounts varied dramatically, mainly because of different methods of balance calculation. Some banking institutions, for example, paid interest only on the "investable balance"—the 88 percent of balances that was not subject to a reserve requirement. Other institutions paid interest only on the lowest balance in accounts over a period of time, often three months. Thus, accounts opened or closed during this period earned no interest.

Since June 23, 1993 (the day the Truth-in-Savings law took effect), banking institutions are required to pay interest on the entire balance in the account for each day. Moreover, institutions are required to disclose the annual percentage yield (APY), which is the percentage interest yield that would be earned on a $100 deposit in one year. This APY, which is described below, and the minimum balance to avoid fees are the two most important factors in determining the yield/cost on savings accounts.

Effective Annual Yield

Effective annual yield is the rate of return that you will earn on your savings provided you do not incur service charges. There are three factors that determine effective annual yield: the interest rate, compounding of interest, and number of days in the bank year.

Interest Rate. In 1992, savings rates fell to levels not seen in decades. By year's end, regular savings accounts were paying, on average, around 2.5 percent. Rates in different areas of the country did not vary a great deal. A December 1992 Consumer Federation of America (CFA) survey of selected institutions revealed a savings rate range of

2.5 to 4.0 percent in the Washington, D.C., area; a range of 2.5 to 3.2 percent in California; and a range of 1.76 to 2.5 percent in Houston. Accordingly, the differences in annual interest earned on balances even as large as $1,000 at different institutions were usually less than $10. Other factors are more important in determining the yield/cost of a regular savings account, such as the minimum balance requirement to earn interest and avoid fees. If balances fall below these levels, savers end up with a net loss on their accounts.

Compounding of Interest. The compounding of interest is, in effect, the practice of paying interest on interest. The more frequently interest is compounded, the greater the effective annual yield.

Continuous compounding is the most favorable method, but it is essentially the same as daily compounding. An account with an average balance of $2,500 will earn only *one cent* more per year under the continuous compounding method as opposed to daily compounding.

Number of Days in the Banking Year. Although there are 365 days in a calendar year, many banks operate on a 360-day year. Some banks and savings and loans divide the rate they pay by 360, but then pay interest for 365 days. This is called compounding on a 365/360 basis, and is the most favorable method to savers. This factor can be more important than the frequency of compounding, as is demonstrated by the following table.

As you can see, the number of days in the bank year is as important as the frequency with which interest is compounded. Semiannual compounding on a 365/360 basis results in the same yield as continuous compounding on a 365/365 basis.

EFFECTIVE ANNUAL YIELD ON ACCOUNTS UNDER
DIFFERENT COMPOUNDING AND BANK-YEAR METHODS

Interest Rate	5.25%	5.25%	5.50%	5.50%
Method	365/365	365/360	365/365	365/360
Semiannual	5.32%	5.39%	5.56%	5.65%
Quarterly	5.35%	5.43%	5.61%	5.69%
Continuously	5.39%	5.47%	5.65%	5.73%

The easiest way to think of effective annual yield is in terms of cents per dollar. A 5.5 percent account compounded continuously on a 365/360 basis pays 5.73 cents per dollar, per year in interest.

❑ Interest on Accounts Closed During Crediting Period

Many financial institutions will not pay interest for a crediting period, the period between the times that an institution actually calculates and posts your interest earnings, if the account is closed during that period. If you have such an account and are contemplating closing it, consider keeping a minimum balance in it until the end of the crediting period.

Accounts that pay interest to the date of closure are clearly preferable to ones that do not. However, since the amount of interest involved is generally small, and the loss of the interest is often avoidable, this is not an important factor.

❑ Minimum Balance to Earn Interest

Many banks and savings and loans have minimum balance requirements for accounts to earn interest. This minimum is applied either to the average balance in the account or to the daily balance. Under the first method, the balances at the end of each day in the interest-crediting period are added together and divided by the number of days. If the result is less than the minimum balance requirement, no interest is earned. Under the second method, if the balance in the account should ever fall below the minimum balance requirement, no interest is earned for the crediting period. A third variation of this requirement is to pay interest only on those days that the minimum balance requirement is met. The last method is the most favorable to most savers; the second method is clearly the least favorable. The first method works out best for those balances that are usually above the minimum even though they occasionally fall below.

CFA's four-city survey revealed that about half of the banks do not have such a requirement. But at several banks, including Chase Manhattan and Chemical in New York City, the minimum balance to earn interest was $500. At a number of California banks, this requirement was $300.

❑ Minimum Balance to Avoid Fees

Most banks require that a minimum balance be kept in your savings account in order to avoid being charged a fee. Usually this balance requirement is several hundred dollars, and the monthly fee is several dollars. But there are exceptions. The CFA survey revealed that in the Washington, D.C., area, Citibank required a minimum of $1,000, and in New York City, Chase Manhattan also required a $1,000 minimum.

Our survey also indicated that a number of banks charge fees as high as $5 per month, and one, Citibank in Washington, D.C., charged $7. Moreover, an increasing number of institutions require that a minimum balance be maintained every three months, and if it is not, assess three months' worth of fees. At Chase Manhattan in New York City that fee is $15.

❑ Other Fees and Charges

Free Accounts for Minors and Older Americans.
Some financial institutions that ordinarily charge fees offer
special no-fee accounts to minors and older persons. Quali-
fied savers should look for accounts with this feature.

Transaction Fees. Some financial institutions limit the
number of withdrawals you can make from your savings account and charge transaction fees for excess withdrawals.
The highest fee we encountered was $3 for each withdrawal
in excess of three per quarter. A more typical charge was $1
per withdrawal in excess of three per quarter. Many institutions do not assess transaction fees. If you intend to make
more than one withdrawal per month, select an institution
that does not assess these fees.

Inactive Account Fees. Some banks and savings and
loans charge fees against accounts if they are completely inactive for a period of time. Such fees are generally levied
against accounts with low balances, and are often designed
to wipe out the account balance before the funds have to be
turned over to the state under abandoned-property laws. By
doing this, institutions avoid the expenses associated with
turning the money over to the state and can retain the funds
for themselves. For example, one bank charges $1.50 per
month after an account has been inactive for sixty days if the
balance was below $50. These charges would wipe out a
$49.50 account in less than three years.

Early Closure Fees. A number of financial institutions
charge a fee if your savings account is closed "early." The
fee is generally modest, $3 or less, and is usually assessed

only if your account is open ninety days or less. Some banks charge considerably more, and some charge the fee if you close the account within one year of opening. The highest fee from our survey was $25 for accounts closed within one year.

C   H   E   C   K   L   I   S   T

Use this checklist when shopping for regular savings accounts.

Minimum balance to open
Minimum balance to earn interest   ____
Annual percentage yield (APY)   ____
Service charges
    ○ Maintenance fee
    ○ Minimum balance to avoid fees   ____
    ○ Transaction fees   ____
    ○ Inactive account fee   ____
    ○ Time period to avoid inactive account fee   ____
    ○ Early closure fee   ____
    ○ Time period to avoid early closure fee   ____

RECOMMENDATIONS

If you cannot afford to set aside at least $1,000 to open a money market account or an account with a money market fund, and you need access to your savings, you should consider a regular savings account. When shopping for a regular savings account at a bank, credit union, or savings and loan, look for the following features:

○ The highest interest rate compounded daily or continuously

○ No or low minimum balance requirements for earning interest and avoiding account maintenance fees

○ No charges for withdrawals unless the number of free withdrawals is greater than the number you reasonably expect to make

○ Accessibility—nearness to your home or work place, convenient hours, and twenty-four-hour teller machines

Investigate credit unions when you consider opening a savings account. They are more likely to have accounts that meet the first three criteria than are banks or savings and loans. Further, many offer free life insurance for the amount of the deposit—typically, up to

$2,000—and often offer higher yields than accounts at other financial institutions.

To keep things in perspective, when shopping for a savings account bear in mind that the difference in interest paid on a $1,000 balance between the highest- and lowest-yielding accounts is less than $20 a year. Factors such as accessibility and fees may prove to be more important to you than yield.

NOTES

5

Savings Bonds and Certificates of Deposit

Frank and Fred held $10,000 CDs from different banks. When the CDs matured, Frank's bank notified him, but Fred's institution did not. And since Fred had forgotten the maturity date and the bank did not automatically renew the CD, his funds sat in the bank earning no interest.

Certificates of Deposit

Certificates of deposit (CDs) are savings accounts that require you to leave your money on deposit for a certain period of time or suffer a penalty. CDs can be offered for any amount, for any time period, and for any rate of interest. As a consequence, and as a result of competition in the marketplace, many institutions will custom-design CDs for their customers. For example, an institution might be willing to offer a 920-day CD to meet customer demand. This feature can be convenient if you are saving for a specific goal. You can either choose a CD that matures exactly when you will need the money or have a CD designed to be worth a desired amount when it matures.

CDs offer several advantages over other long-term savings options:

O   They are easy to buy and involve no brokerage fees or other transaction costs.

O   They are insured by an agency of the federal government for up to $100,000 per customer per institution if the issuing institution is insured (and most are).

O   They are relatively easy to understand.

O   There are rarely any management fees for IRAs set up as CDs.

CDs, however, also have disadvantages. These include the following:

○ They are nonliquid. Except when purchased from a broker who buys and sells them, a CD of less than $100,000 can be redeemed for cash only by the issuing institution. There are usually penalties for early withdrawals, and the issuer is under no obligation to permit such withdrawals.

○ Searching for the best yield on a CD can be time-consuming.

○ Yields are generally somewhat lower than on riskier investment options.

❑ **Factors Affecting Yield**

Yields on CDs vary widely, both from institution to institution and from city to city. In fact, one survey revealed one savings and loan that paid higher yields at its branches in some cities than in others.

Surveys reveal that the effective annual yield ranges about one percentage point in each area and two percentage points nationwide for CDs of different maturities. What these differences mean in dollars is revealed by a ten-city survey published in the August 1988 issue of <u>Consumer Reports</u>. On a ninety-day, $1,500 CD, net earnings ranged from $20.01 to $27.73. On a five-year, $1,500 CD, net earnings varied from $607.35 to $819.56.

Rates. Advertising practices of financial institutions make interest rate comparisons difficult, because of the different ways in which interest can be stated. An example of potentially misleading advertising of interest rates was an advertisement that offered a simple interest rate of 15 percent on a five-year CD. Since the interest on this CD was not compounded, it would pay less than a CD with an annual rate of 11.5 percent compounded daily.

Most consumers should concentrate on effective annual yield. However, if you choose a CD that pays interest monthly, you should pay attention to rates, since on these CDs interest usually is not compounded. The only reliable way to compare income option CDs is to determine the size of the monthly or quarterly interest payments.

Above certain levels, some banking institutions pay higher interest rates. They may, for example, pay a higher rate on a $50,000 CD than on a $500 one. But the greatest variation in rates reflects the length of time you are prepared to tie up your money. In December 1992, according to "100 Highest Yields and Jumbo Flash Report," average rates for different types of CDs were as follows:

6-month:	3.05%
1-year:	3.35%
2.5-year:	4.10%
5-year:	5.46%

Compounding. Compounding is the paying of interest on interest; it raises the effective annual yield of an investment. For a given rate, the more frequent the compounding, the higher the effective annual yield.

Most banking institutions compound daily, but not all do. In a 1992 survey of CDs offered by California institutions, Consumer Action found that many compound monthly, while several compound quarterly, and several did not compound at all. CDs with no compounding are usually not worth the investment.

The following table demonstrates the impact of compounding on the amount of interest earned on a $10,000, one-year CD paying 10 percent.

IMPACT OF DIFFERENT METHODS OF COMPOUNDING

Type of Compounding	Interest Earned
Simple (no compounding)	$1000.00
Semiannual	$1025.00
Quarterly	$1038.13
Monthly	$1047.13
Daily	$1051.56
Continuously	$1051.71

Days in the Bank Year. Although there are 365 days in a calendar year, there are only 360 days in the bank year at most institutions. Yet a few institutions pay interest for 365 days even though they only have 360 days in their bank year. This practice, called compounding on a 365/360 basis, raises the effective annual yield of an account by a factor of 0.0139.

This practice is an artifact of the days when banks were subject to maximums on the annual rate of interest they could pay. Compounding on a 365/360-day basis was used to raise effective annual yields without exceeding the maximum annual rate.

❑ Other Features of CDs

Minimum to Open Account. For the past decade, some banks have increased the minimum amount that you can deposit in a CD. At many institutions, this minimum remains $500. But at others, it is considerably higher. A 1992 Consumer Action survey of California banks revealed minimums of $2,500 at a number of institutions and a minimum of $5,000 at two.

Mailing of Interest and Interest Transfers. If you purchase a CD for income, there are two convenient ways to receive the interest earnings—have interest checks mailed to you or have the interest transferred to another account at the same institution. If you have a short-term CD that does not compound interest, you should have the interest mailed to you as frequently as possible and deposit the proceeds in an interest-bearing account, since you will earn no interest on the funds accumulating in your CD.

On CDs with maturities of one year or more, most institutions offer both options. The great majority of institutions also offer both options on six-month CDs. Many institutions, however, offer these options only on CDs above a minimum amount as high as $100,000. However, typical minimums are $5,000 for monthly payments and $1,000 for quarterly payments.

Notice of Maturing CD. Look for institutions that will send you a notice when your CD is about to mature. Most will do it automatically. But a minority send notices only if the rates paid on their CDs have changed since the CD was first issued. Without notification, it is easy to forget the exact maturity date of a long-term CD, and there may be adverse consequences for letting a matured CD sit.

Unless you instruct an institution to the contrary, most will automatically renew your CD for the same term at the current rate when it matures. Many will allow you to elect an automatic renewal option at the time you purchase the CD. Although this may seem desirable, it has two disadvantages. You may unknowingly receive a lower yield than you could earn elsewhere. What's more, if your CD has already been renewed at a time when you need the principal, you will be assessed early-withdrawal penalties.

Most institutions that do not automatically renew maturing CDs pay no interest on the deposited funds after the maturity date.

Renewal of Maturing CDs. Redeem your CD on the day it matures and reinvest your funds, if appropriate, at the highest yield you can find at an insured institution. If possible, arrange ahead of time to have the proceeds from a maturing CD transferred to an interest-bearing account on the maturity date.

Early-Withdrawal Penalties. Most banks and savings and loans charge a substantial penalty for early withdrawals from CDs. The minimum is one month's simple interest on the amount withdrawn for CDs with a maturity of one year or less, and three months' interest for those with longer terms. These penalties can be waived by the issuer.

Early-withdrawal penalties can exceed the interest earnings on your account. If this happens, you will not receive any interest, and will lose part of your principal as well.

Less than one-half of the institutions we surveyed charged the federal minimum penalties. Most charge substantially more, and some use replacement cost when that is more than the federal minimum as the basis for their penalties. The most common method for assessing replacement cost is to compute the additional interest cost to the institution of issuing a new CD for the term remaining on the CD being cashed in early. For example, if you want to cash in a three-year 12 percent CD after one year, and the current rate for two-year CDs is 14 percent, the replacement cost would be 4 percent of the face value (2 percent times two years). On a $10,000 certificate, your penalty would be $400. This is $100 more than the federal minimum penalty of three months' interest.

A replacement-cost penalty is equitable inasmuch as it compensates the institution for the additional expense involved in replacing funds the depositor had committed for an agreed-upon time. However, institutions using replacement-cost penalties should not also subject their depositors to federal minimums. In fact, we believe that institutions should pay a bonus for early withdrawals if interest rates have fallen, since the issuers can replace the funds at a lower interest rate.

Most institutions that do not use replacement cost and/or federal minimums in computing early-withdrawal penalties charge three months' interest for CDs with terms of one year or less, and six months' interest on CDs with terms of over one year. These are the old federal minimums. Some institutions, however, assess penalties that are harsher than the old federal penalties. For example, one Washington, D.C., institution charges six months' interest on a one-year certificate of deposit.

If you are considering cashing in a CD early, you should explore other ways to raise the money you need. One alternative is to borrow funds from the issuer of the CD, using the certificate as collateral. Such loans are sometimes available at an interest rate only one or two percentage points above the rate being paid on the CD. In some cases, especially when the CD is close to maturity, an installment loan or even a cash advance on a credit card would be less costly than cashing in a CD early.

❑ Where to Find High-Yield CDs

Bank Rate Monitor publishes a monthly newsletter, *100 Highest Yields*, that lists some of the highest rated CDs of different maturities. The business section of the Sunday *New York Times* gives a sample of these certificates of deposit. The January 24, 1993, edition lists the following rates.

EXAMPLES OF HIGH-RATE CDS (JANUARY 1993)

6-Month CDs	Yield
Southern Pacific T&L, Culver City, Calif.	3.82%
Citibank/SD, Sioux Falls, S. Dak.	3.78%
First Dep. National Bank, Tilton, N.H.	3.76%
Continental Savings of America, San Francisco, Calif.	3.75%
First Bank of Beverly Hills, Beverly Hills, Calif.	3.75%

1-Year CDs	
Treasure Land S&L, Ontario, Ore.	4.19%
J C Penney National Bank, Harrington, Del.	4.15%
First Dep. National Bank, Tilton, N.H.	4.11%
California Thrift & Loan, Santa Barbara, Calif.	4.11%
Key Bank USA, Albany, N.Y.	4.07%

2.5-Year CDs	
J C Penney National Bank, Harrington, Del.	5.20%
First Dep. National Bank, Tilton, N.H.	5.19%
Citibank/SD, Sioux Falls, S. Dak.	5.18%
California Thrift & Loan, Santa Barbara, Calif.	5.15%
Key Bank USA, Albany, N.Y.	5.12%

5-Year CDs	
Treasure Land S&L, Ontario, Ore.	6.27%
First Family Bank, Eustis, Fla.	6.25%
California Thrift & Loan, Santa Barbara, Calif.	6.20%
Key Bank USA, Albany, N.Y.	6.17%
Columbia First Bank, Arlington, Va.	6.15%

❑ Variable-Rate CDs

Some banking institutions offer some sort of variable-rate CD, although most of these institutions issue them only for IRAs. IRA CDs generally require very low initial deposits—as little as $1 but typically $100—and allow or require additional investments during the term of the certificate. The highest initial deposit we found for an IRA was $500. Minimum additions ranged from a low of $1 to a high of $100.

Non-IRA variable-rate CDs usually require initial investments of at least $500. The typical term for a variable-rate CD is eighteen months, but some institutions offer terms as short as three months.

The majority of institutions offering variable-rate CDs change the rate monthly. Some adjust rates weekly, and a few change rates daily.

At most institutions interest rate adjustments on variable-rate CDs are left to the discretion of management. This is not favorable to consumers, and it is best to avoid such accounts. Other institutions tie the rate to rates on other products they offer. For example, several banks tie the rate to what they pay on newly issued six-month CDs.

Most other institutions set the rate on their variable-rate CDs according to either the thirteen-week or twenty-six-week Treasury bill auction rate. The auction rate is a discount rate and is considerably less than the actual yield of these instruments. Several institutions paid a premium of as much as one percentage point above the auction rate.

In brief, look for a variable-rate CD with a high yield that is indexed to some federal interest rate. Such an index will prevent the bank from arbitrarily lowering the rate.

U.S. Savings Bonds (Series EE)

For years, U.S. savings bonds were a poor choice for savers. They paid a lower rate of interest than savings accounts and were less liquid. Early redemption dates were spaced six months apart, and when savers cashed their bonds in early, they lost any interest they would have earned following an early redemption date.

The principal advantages of savings bonds were that they could be purchased in small denominations and that they received more favorable tax treatment than ordinary savings. Savings bond interest is exempt from state and local taxes, and federal taxes on earnings are deferred until the bonds are cashed.

The basic change in savings bonds that makes them worth considering today is that they now pay a reasonable rate of interest. If you hold savings bonds for at least five years, they will earn 85 percent of the average yield on five-year Treasuries during their lifetime, with a minimum guaranteed rate of 6 percent in early 1993. The rate of earnings is adjusted every six months.

If you cash your savings bonds in earlier than five years after issue, they will earn considerably less interest. If you cash them in after one year, they would pay 4.2 percent. Every six months the rate of earnings is increased, so a bond held two and one-half years would pay 4.8 percent. All interest is compounded semiannually.

Although savings bonds usually do not pay as much as long-term CDs—the end of 1992 was an unusual period—you should consider them if you are a small saver. They are particularly suitable if you can set aside only small sums of money on a regular basis for a goal in the distant future.

The tax advantages of savings bonds are unlikely to be of much use to most of the savers for whom the bonds are a reasonable savings alternative. This is because savings bonds are most appropriate for relatively low-income, low-tax-bracket savers.

Further, if savers are not careful, the tax-deferral feature may result in higher taxes. This would almost certainly be the case for a child who accumulates a significant number of savings bonds for a college education. If all or many of the bonds are cashed in the same year, the accumulated interest that was deferred for tax purposes is likely to result in a significant income tax liability.

There are two ways to avoid this liability. One is to declare the interest earned each year on your income tax statement. The second is to try to take advantage of a relatively new federal program available to low- and middle-income families. Couples with an annual adjusted gross income of up to $60,000 and singles earning up to $40,000 can purchase series EE bonds with the interest accumulating free of taxes as long as the proceeds are later used to pay college tuition. A partial sliding scale is allowed for couples earning up to $90,000 and singles earning up to $55,000.

C H E C K L I S T

Use this checklist when shopping for CDs.

Minimum size
Interest rate   _____
Method of compounding   _____
Days in bank year   _____
Yield   _____
Are additions allowed?
   ○ Without extending term   _____
   ○ With extending term   _____
Size of quarterly or monthly check
(income option only)   _____
Notice of maturing CD sent?   _____
If not instructions at maturity, what is done?   _____
Early-withdrawal penalty   _____
For variable-rate CDs
   ○ Frequency of rate adjustment   _____
   ○ Is rate tied to an index?   _____
   ○ Minimum addition (if available)   _____

R E C O M M E N D A T I O N S

Certificates of deposit (CDs) are appropriate investments if you are willing to give up access to your funds, but are unwilling to assume any risk of default. When purchasing a CD, aggressively seek out the highest yield, even if you find it in another city. CDs can be purchased and redeemed by mail, and require no attention in between.

To maximize interest earned, purchase an investment option CD, in which interest is not paid out periodically, but accumulates until maturity. Shop for this type of CD by comparing the effective annual yields offered by different institutions. Be aware, however, that you must pay income taxes on the interest earnings of such a CD each year even though you will not receive the interest until maturity. The only exceptions to this rule are CDs with a maturity of one year or less and those representing IRAs. With these CDs, you can defer taxes until the interest is actually paid.

If you wish to receive interest earnings periodically, you should choose the income option CD. Under this option, monthly or quarterly interest payments will be made by the issuing institution, either by check or by transfer to another account. The only reliable way to shop for such a CD is to determine what the size of the monthly or quarterly interest will be.

If you do not want to lock yourself into a fixed rate of interest for a long period of time, you should consider variable-rate CDs. Most of these are designed for individual retirement accounts (IRAs). Many require very low initial investments and allow funds to be added to the principal at any time.

No matter what type of CD you choose, avoid those with high early-withdrawal penalties if there is any chance that a withdrawal will be made.

NOTES

6

Money Market Accounts and Money Market Funds

Sarah and Simone each had $10,000 to invest, but wanted easy access to their money without having to pay a penalty for a withdrawal. Sarah chose a money market account, and Simone selected a money market fund. Sarah earned $10 less on her deposit in one year than did Simone, but Sarah felt that her funds were a little more secure than if they had been deposited in a money market fund.

If you have significant amounts to save, two liquid savings options that in most periods pay competitive interest rates are available to you: money market accounts (MMAs) at banks and savings and loans, and money market funds (MMFs). The most important differences between the two accounts are typical yield and risk. In the low-interest-rate environment of early 1993, the average MMA paid about one-tenth of a percentage point less than the average MMF. When interest rates are higher, the spread increases to several tenths of a percentage point.

MMAs, like other deposits at most banks and savings and loans, are insured by agencies of the federal government for up to $100,000. Although MMFs have proven to be very safe, they are not federally insured and therefore carry some risk.

Money Market Accounts (MMAs)

Since December 1982, federal regulations have allowed banks, savings and loans, and credit unions to offer MMAs to compete effectively for the more than $200 billion that had flowed into money market funds during the late 1970s and early 1980s. Institutions may pay any interest rate they wish on MMAs and change the rate as often as they desire without informing the depositor. On average, the yield on these accounts is slightly below the yields that can be earned from MMFs.

MMAs are subject to restrictions mandated by federal regulations. Although check writing and automatic transfers are allowed, there are limits to the number of such transactions. No more than a total of six such transactions is allowed in any given month, with no more than three of these transactions in the form of checks. If these totals are regularly exceeded, the regulators consider the account to be a transactions account rather than an MMA, and the issuing institutions are subject to high reserve requirements on the balances in the accounts.

Banks and savings and loans have taken several different steps to discourage or prevent customers from exceeding the limits on checks and automatic transfers. Most charge a hefty fee for excess transactions. The typical fee is between $5 and $10; however, banks can charge as much as $25 and as little as $1. Others simply close the consumer's account if excess transactions continue. Still others refuse to honor checks written in excess of the limit and refuse to make preauthorized or telephone transfers. As an additional penalty, the depositor is usually charged a bounced-check fee.

Since there is always the chance you may inadvertently exceed your check limit, avoid accounts that either charge high excess-transaction fees or dishonor checks written in excess of the limit. If you regularly exceed transaction limits, you should seriously consider an MMF or a NOW account as an alternative.

❑ **Factors to Consider in Choosing an MMA**

Annual Percentage Yield (APY). Since late June 1993, banking institutions have been required to disclose the annual percentage yield (APY) on all MMAs, which is the percentage interest yield that would be earned on a $100 deposit in one year. The two important factors that determine this yield are the rate of interest and the method of compounding.

The rate of interest paid on MMAs can vary widely. A 1988 *Consumer Reports* survey revealed that rates, at institutions in ten cities, ranged from 4 to 7 percent. A 1992 Consumer Action survey of California institutions found that, on a deposit of $2,500, rates varied from 2.25 to 4.75 percent (the latter at two credit unions). In early 1993, rates were even lower, the range even smaller. But it is still worthwhile to pay attention to them. *Bank Rate Monitor* re-

ported in January 1993 that the average rate was 2.7 percent, but that rates went as high as 4 percent.

What is the difference between the yield on one MMA
paying 2 percent and another paying 4 percent? Without
compounding, the 2 percent account will yield $20 on a
$1,000 deposit while the 4 percent account will yield $40.
On much larger accounts, the differences are significant—
$200 versus $400 when $10,000 is on deposit.

In general, banking institutions do not compound interest as generously on MMAs as they do on regular savings
accounts. In Consumer Action's California survey, institutions typically compounded monthly. But, as noted in chapter 4, unless very large sums are on deposit, the difference
between daily and monthly compounding involves small
amounts. For example, on a $10,000 deposit, this difference
is less than $5 in one year.

Minimum Balance to Avoid Fees. As they do for
checking and regular savings accounts, most banking institutions require that a minimum balance be maintained on
MMAs, or fees are levied. The difference is that for MMAs
the minimums are usually much higher than on the other
two accounts. At about one-half the California institutions
surveyed by Consumer Action in 1992, the minimum balance requirement was at least $2,500. At several institutions
it was $5,000. On the other hand, at several
institutions—including more than half the credit unions
surveyed—there were no minimums and no fees.

When minimums are not met, substantial fees are
charged. At nearly all the California institutions with fees
surveyed by Consumer Action, these charges were between
$5 and $10 per month. A $10 monthly fee offsets the inter-
est earned on $4,000 paying 3 percent interest. Since many

accounts average less than this, it is not difficult, on MMAs, to pay more in fees than interest earned. Thus, it is essential to select an MMA with a minimum balance requirement that can be met.

Minimum Balance to Earn Interest or a Higher Rate. At a few institutions, a substantial minimum balance must be maintained, not just to avoid fees but also to earn interest. At many, however, above a certain minimum balance, a higher rate is paid. Typically, according to the 1988 *Consumer Reports* survey, the difference in rate was only several tenths of a percentage point. Yet, at a few institutions the difference exceeded one percentage point.

Method of Computing Interest. As explained in chapter 4, before passage of Truth-in-Savings legislation in late 1992, yields on savings accounts, including money market accounts, varied dramatically mainly because of different methods of balance calculation. Now, however, banking institutions are required to pay interest on the entire balance in the account for each day.

Interest on Accounts Closed During Crediting Period. Many institutions do not pay interest on accounts closed during a crediting period, which is always a month, but not necessarily a calendar month. Some do so only at the personal request of the customer.

If you are planning to switch accounts from an institution that does not pay interest when an account is closed, you should wait until the end of the interest-crediting period to do so. Any advantages of your new account are likely to be more than offset by the interest lost on your old account.

❑ Transactions in MMAs

Deposits. Most institutions allow unlimited deposits of any size to their MMAs. There are exceptions, however. A number of institutions require that deposits be at least $100, and a few set the minimum even higher, as high as $500 in a CFA survey several years ago.

Withdrawals and Transfers. You can gain access to the funds in your money market account in several different ways. Withdrawals can be made at teller windows or ATMs. Funds can also be transferred by personal check, telephone transfer to another account, or preauthorized transfer to pay bills. Federal regulations limit these indirect transfers to six a month, with a maximum of three third-party checks included in that total.

Financial institutions differ widely in their policies on minimum transaction size and maximum number of transactions. Most allow an unlimited number of deposits and direct withdrawals, and allow the legal limit on indirect transfers, with no minimum size, and charge no fees. This is the most favorable policy to savers, and you should seek it out.

Several institutions require a minimum size on direct withdrawals. The highest minimum in a 1985 CFA survey was $500.

All the financial institutions surveyed allowed some in-person withdrawals at no charge, as long as minimum balance requirements were met. However, some institutions levied a charge for on-premise ATM withdrawals or for all ATM transactions.

Several institutions limit the number of free withdrawals that can be made from MMAs. One bank charged $3 per withdrawal in excess of three per month; however, it exempted

ATM transactions from this limit. Others had higher limits or lower fees.

Accounts that allow unlimited free withdrawals are preferable to those that do not. Since most savers make few withdrawals from MMAs, a restriction on the number of withdrawals does not seriously limit the usefulness of these accounts.

Money Market Funds (MMFs)

Money market funds were first introduced in 1972, but became popular with consumers only in the late 1970s when interest rates soared. They invest in a variety of short-term securities that earn market rates of interest. After a portion of the earnings is retained as a management fee (generally between 0.5 and 0.75 percent), these earnings are credited to the shareholders.

The funds maintain the value of a share at $1, so that an MMF account works very much like a bank account—a purchase of 1,000 shares costs $1,000. Earnings are paid in shares, rather than allowing the value of a share to increase. So if you invested $1,000 in a fund for one year, and earnings averaged 10 percent, at the end of the year you would own 1,100 shares worth $1,100.

MMFs work in very much the same way as MMAs at banks. Deposits and withdrawals may be made at any time, and there are minimum transaction sizes and minimum balance requirements.

☐ **Advantages and Disadvantages over MMAs**
MMFs offer the following advantages over MMAs:

1. You can open an account with an initial deposit of only
    $1,000 and sometimes only $500, although there are
    some funds that require deposits of $100,000. On the other
    hand, many funds have lower minimums for IRA accounts.

2. Most funds charge no fees of any kind except for wire
    transfers and the built-in management fee.

3. Minimum balance requirements for keeping your ac-
    count open are usually only $500, and as little as $1 at
    some funds. If your account does not meet the require
    ment, it is merely closed after sixty days and the balance
    is mailed to you. Your account continues to earn inter-
    est until it is closed.

    MMFs have the following disadvantages compared to MMAs:

1. They are not insured by an agency of the federal govern-
    ment. In fact, they are usually not insured at all, and are
    therefore riskier than accounts at federally insured
    banks, savings and loans, and credit unions.

2. They are not as accessible as accounts at local financial
    institutions. In order to withdraw money, you must
    make a phone call, write a check, or write a letter to
    the fund.

3. They are more difficult to evaluate than accounts at
    financial institutions. You must not only compare yields
    and features but also evaluate the risk of each fund that
    you are considering. Funds that invest in short-term se-
    curities are safer than those investing in longer term
    securities.

❑ MMFs Available to General Public

There are four types of money market funds available to the general public.

General-Purpose Funds. These are the most common types of funds. They invest in a variety of money market instruments, such as large corporate CDs and government securities.

Government-only Funds. These invest only in securities issued by the federal government or its agencies. Government-only funds are somewhat safer than general-purpose funds. Most, however, invest in repurchase agreements that are backed by government securities, so are not as safe as the securities themselves.

Funds Exempt from Federal Income Tax. These invest primarily in obligations of state and local governments that are exempt from federal income taxes. They are recommended for individuals in the highest income tax bracket.

Funds Exempt from Both Federal and State Income Taxes. These invest primarily in municipal securities issued by governments within the state for which they were designed. They are suitable for individuals in a combined federal and state income tax bracket of over 40 percent.

With the exception of the investments that they make and the customers they are designed for, all of the funds work in about the same way. In order to open an account, you must first request a prospectus, as required by federal security laws. You must then fill out a simple application form and either mail or wire a minimum initial investment to the fund.

❑ Withdrawals

There are several ways that you can withdraw money. The easiest and most popular method is to write a check to either yourself or a third party. Almost all funds provide this service. Minimum check size ranges from no minimum (with cash management accounts) to $500. Most funds require a minimum check size of $500. A few non-CMA funds require only $250.

A second way to withdraw funds is through telephone transfer. Under this method, money is either transferred by wire to your checking account or mailed to you by check. Many funds charge a nominal wire-transfer fee, generally about $5.

A third way to withdraw funds is by sending a form to the fund, which they will provide, requesting a withdrawal. This method is generally used only to close an account.

Finally, many funds have systematic withdrawal programs. Under this method, a monthly or quarterly check of specified size will be mailed to you. Funds providing this service often require that you keep a minimum balance of $5,000 or $10,000, and often require a minimum systematic withdrawal of at least $25. This method of withdrawal is especially good for IRAs in the withdrawal stage.

❑ Evaluating the Risk of Money Market Funds

Although they are reasonably safe, MMFs are not insured by agencies of the federal government and therefore do involve some risk. There are three types of risk that depositors in money market funds are exposed to: market, solvency, and default.

Market risk is the possibility that the securities in which a fund invests will fall in value. This would happen if interest rates rose. The funds protect themselves from this risk by maintaining investment portfolios that have very short average maturity lengths. Most funds have an average maturity of between thirty and sixty days. The average maturity length for any fund will fluctuate with the interest rate forecasts that management makes. If management thinks that rates are about to fall, it will generally lengthen the average maturity of the fund's portfolio. Conversely, if it thinks rates will rise, the average maturity length will be shortened. Usually, funds do not sell their securities; they wait for them to mature.

A fund may experience a sudden run by its depositors and be unable to pay everybody on demand. This is solvency risk. The shorter the maturity length of a fund's portfolio, the lower the solvency risk. Funds have two other protections against insolvency. First, they can legally make their shareholders wait for up to seven days for payment. Second, funds are allowed to borrow against their assets.

Risk of default is the possibility that one of the issuers of an obligation that a fund holds will not repay its debt. To protect against this, funds invest only in very high-grade debt instruments. Nevertheless, some funds make investments that are riskier than others in order to realize a higher yield. The most common investments made by funds are listed below.

Treasury Securities. These are obligations of the U.S. Treasury. They are backed by the full faith and credit of the federal government and are absolutely free of risk of default, but they are the lowest-yielding assets held by funds.

Agency Securities. These are obligations of agencies of the U.S. government, such as the Small Business Administration. Many of these securities are only moral obligations of the federal government and are not backed by its full faith and credit. While it is unlikely that Congress would ever allow a government agency to default on its obligations, delays are possible. These securities yield several tenths of a percentage point more than Treasury securities.

Domestic Bank CDs. Only the first $100,000 of each of these CDs is insured. Since they are often issued in denominations of tens of millions of dollars, they involve some risk of default. Funds generally limit themselves to purchasing CDs from major commercial banks and savings and loans. Since federal regulators have shown that they are loath to allow a major financial institution to collapse, these investments are quite safe. Further, funds monitor the financial health of these institutions closely. For example, the funds liquidated their positions in Continental Illinois CDs at least six months prior to that bank's near collapse. Domestic bank CDs pay about 0.75 percent more than do Treasury securities.

Banker's Acceptances. These instruments are similar to a postdated check that is authorized (accepted) by a major commercial bank. Banker's acceptances are used primarily in international trade. Those issued by U.S. banks have about the same risk and offer the same yield as domestic CDs.

Letters of Credit. Similar to banker's acceptances, these instruments authorize a foreign correspondent of a U.S. bank to pay the holder funds. They have about the same risk and yield as banker's acceptances.

Eurodollar CDs. These are obligations of foreign branches of U.S. banks that are denominated in dollars.

These CDs expose funds to political risk. For example, a country could impose currency controls, making it impossible for the foreign branch to pay its obligations. These are riskier but yield several tenths of a percentage point more than domestic bank CDs.

Yankee CDs. These are issued by the U.S. branches of foreign banks. They have about the same risk and yield as do Eurodollar CDs.

Commercial Paper. These are the short-term, unsecured debts of major domestic corporations. The best commercial paper is rated A-1 by Standard & Poor's and P-1 by Moody's. The lowest rated paper any fund will invest in is rated A-3 or P-3, which means that the rating services think that the issuer has only a satisfactory capacity for timely repayment. Most funds will not buy commercial paper rated lower than A-2 or P-2. The highest rated commercial paper has about the same yield as domestic bank CDs. A-3 and P-3 paper yields about one percentage point more than does A-1 or P-1 paper.

Repurchase Agreements (Repos). Under these arrangements, funds buy securities, usually Treasury securities, with an agreement that the original owner will buy them back at a given time, usually the next day, at an agreed-upon price. The difference between the two prices represents the interest the fund earns on the arrangement. Since the securities involved may never leave the possession of the original owner, repos can be construed as a secured loan rather than an outright sale. If the issuer goes bankrupt while the repo is in force, the fund will have to wait in line with other creditors to recover the securities. Consequently, repos are not as safe as the securities that underlie them.

Some government-only funds invest heavily in repos. In fact, the Reserve Fund's government-only money market fund was 100 percent invested in repos at the time its last annual report was issued.

Municipals. These are generally the obligations of state and local governments. Only tax-exempt funds invest in them. Municipals are also rated by the services, with the highest quality issues rated AAA and Aaa. The lowest grade municipal that most funds will invest in is rated AA or Aa.

❑ Choosing a Money Market Fund

When choosing a money market fund, you should consider the yield it offers, the convenience of its special features (such as minimum deposits), and the risk you are willing to take. The first step is to obtain prospectuses and annual reports from each fund that you are considering, and evaluate them carefully. Then compare yields over several years of a number of funds. This information is usually contained in the annual reports and publications of various reporting services available in many libraries. Ask the reference librarian for information about these publications.

An especially useful source is *IBC/Donoghue's Money Fund Directory*, available for $29.95 by calling 1-800-343-5413 or writing to: 290 Eliot St., Box 91004, Ashland, MA 01721-9104. Among other information, this book lists the largest and top-performing money market funds with their twelve-month total return, minimum initial and subsequent investment amounts, and minimum checks that can be written, if available.

30 LARGEST MONEY MARKET MUTUAL FUNDS (12-31-92)

Fund (by rank)	Return	Initial	Subsequent	Check
Merrill Lynch CMA MF	3.52%	$ 5,000	$ 0	$ 500
American Express Daily Dividend	3.52%	$ 2,500	$1,000	NA
Vanguard MMR/Prime Port.	3.74%	$ 3,000	$ 100	$ 250
Fidelity Cash Reserves	3.75%	$ 2,500	$ 250	$ 500
Dean Witter/Sears Liquid Asset	3.37%	$ 5,000	$ 100	$ 500
CMA Tax-Exempt MF	2.60%	$ 5,000	$ 0	$ 500
Merrill Lynch Ready Assets	3.45%	$ 5,000	$1,000	$ 500
Prudential MoneyMart Assets	3.58%	$ 1,000	$ 100	$ 500
Schwab MMF	3.47%	$ 1,000	$ 100	NA
Dreyfus Liquid Assets	3.47%	$ 2,500	$ 100	$ 500
Dreyfus Worldwide Dollar MMF	3.81%	$ 2,500	$ 100	$ 500
Kemper MMF/Money Market Port.	3.51%	$ 1,000	$ 100	$ 500
Fidelity Spartan MMF	3.97%	$20,000	$1,000	$1,000
Daily Cash Accumulation Fund	3.53%	$ 500	$ 25	$ 250
PaineWebber RMA MF/MM Port.	3.56%	$ 0	$ 0	$ 0
Merrill Lynch CMA Gov't Securities	3.45%	$ 5,000	$ 0	$ 500
American Express Municipal MM	2.67%	$ 500	$ 250	$ 250
PaineWebber CASHFUND	3.54%	$ 5,000	$ 500	$ 500
T. Rowe Price Prime Reserve	3.36%	$ 2,500	$ 100	$ 500
Dean Witter/Active Assets MT	3.47%	$10,000	$ 0	NA
Cash Equivalent Fund/MM Port	3.17%	$ 1,000	$ 100	$ 250
American Express Gov't & Agencies	3.50%	$ 2,500	$1,000	NA
Vanguard Muni Bond/MMP	3.01%	$ 3,000	$ 100	$ 250
Smith Barney Cash Port.	3.31%	$ 1,500	$ 100	$ 500
Capital Preservation Fund	3.29%	$ 1,000	$ 100	$ 100
Cash Equivalent Fund/Gov't Securities	3.18%	$ 1,000	$ 100	$ 250
Dreyfus 100% U.S. Treas. MMF LP	3.64%	$ 2,500	$ 100	$ 500
Fidelity Tax-Exempt MM Trust	2.88%	$ 5,000	$ 500	$ 0
Fidelity Daily Income Trust	3.59%	$ 5,000	$ 500	NA
Daily Passport Cash Trust	3.04%	$ 1,000	$1,000	$ 500

TOP-PERFORMING GOVERNMENT FUNDS (12-31-92)

Fund	Return	Initial	Subsequent	Check
United Services Gov't Sec. Savings	4.43%	$ 1,000	$ 50	$ 500
Blanchard 100% Treas. MMF	3.88%	$ 1,000	$ 200	$ 250
Mariner Gov't MMF	3.80%	$ 1,000	$ 50	$ 500
Fidelity Spartan U.S. Gov't MMF	3.77%	$20,000	$1,000	$1,000
Parkstone U.S. Gov't Obligations	3.72%	$ 1,000	$ 0	NA
Strong U.S. Treas. Money Fund	3.72%	$ 1,000	$ 50	$ 500
Transamer. U.S. Gov't Cash Resrs.	3.70%	$20,000	$ 500	$ 500
Fidelity Spartan U.S. Treas. MMF	3.68%	$20,000	$1,000	$1,000
Vanguard MMR Federal Port.	3.68%	$ 3,000	$ 100	$ 250
Salem Treas. MMF/Trust	3.67%	$ 1,000	$ 0	NA

TOP-PERFORMING GENERAL-PURPOSE FUNDS (12-31-92)

Fund	Return	Initial	Subsequent	Check
Riverside Capital MMF	3.98%	$1,000	$50	NA
Fidelity Spartan MMF	3.97%	$25,000	$1,000	$1,000
Alger MM Port.	3.93%	$1,000	$100	$500
Cowen Standby Reserve Fund	3.89%	$2,000	$500	$100
Evergreen MM Trust	3.88%	$2,000	$100	$500
Dreyfus Worldwide Dollar MMF	3.81%	$2,500	$100	$500
USAA MM Fund	3.80%	$1,000	$50	$250
Sierra Global Money Fund	3.79%	$1,000	$100	$500
Prime Value Cash Investment Fund	3.79%	$100,000	$0	$500
Mariner Cash Management Fund	3.77%	$1,000	$50	$500

C   H   E   C   K   L   I   S   T

Use this checklist when shopping for MMAs.

Minimum opening balance   _____
Minimum balance to earn high interest   _____
How is balance computed?   _____
Average yield last year   _____
Current yield   _____
Is rate paid tied to an index?   _____
Minimum deposit   _____
Minimum check   _____
Minimum withdrawal   _____
Maximum number of withdrawals
  ○   By check   _____
  ○   By transfer   _____
  ○   Direct   _____
Service charges
  ○   Account maintenance fee   _____
  ○   Minimum balance to avoid fee   _____
  ○   Regular transaction fees   _____

Use this checklist when shopping for MMFs.

Minimum initial investment   _____
Minimum additional investment   _____
Minimum check size   _____
Minimum balance   _____
Average yield last year   _____
Most recent yield   _____
Investments authorized by prospectus   _____
Other services available   _____
Fees
  ○   Excess transaction fees   _____
  ○   Other (e.g., balance inquiry)   _____

R E C O M M E N D A T I O N S

If you have more than $1,000 in savings and want ready access to your money, keep your savings in either a money market fund (MMF) or a money market account (MMA). The choice between the two is a difficult one. MMFs offer a somewhat higher yield, provide unlimited check writing (usually subject to a minimum check size), and are generally free of fees, but are not federally insured. MMAs offer only limited check-writing privileges (usually three checks per month) and often charge fees, but are more accessible than MMFs and carry federal insurance.

To earn the maximum yield on an MMA, it is essential to meet minimum or average balance requirements to avoid fees. At most banking institutions, the minimum ranges from $1,000 to $2,500, but at a few—including many credit unions—it is lower or does not exist. Look also for MMAs that compound daily or continuously.

Savers who choose MMFs have a broader range of choices. The ideal MMF has conservative investments, low transaction minimums, offers a toll-free number for transfers, and has no fees. The cost of greater safety and convenience may be a slightly lower yield than other funds pay. When shopping for an MMF, compromises often must be made.

7

Mutual Funds
and Annuities

*Charlene recently had a certificate of deposit (CD)
mature that was earning 8 percent interest. When she
went to the bank to renew it, she was appalled to discover that the best CD rate available was 3 percent.
Although she had not planned on putting her money
into anything other than a CD, this very low rate
forced her to search for alternative products. After
consulting friends and family members who were
knowledgeable about financial products, she put her
money into a mutual fund where she hopes to earn
anywhere from 7 to 10 percent on her investment.*

*Dave wants to put a percentage of his salary
from a new job into a savings account to assist him
during retirement. But, because he is in a high tax
bracket, he does not want to have to pay additional
taxes on the interest he will earn. After evaluating
various products available to him, he opts for a tax
deferred annuity through which his interest earnings
will grow tax-free until he begins to make withdrawals upon retirement.*

The average interest paid on six-month CDs in mid-
1993 was 3.01 percent, down from 3.95 percent a year earlier and 6.72 percent just two years earlier. In this low-interest-rate environment, many people are abandoning their
deposit accounts in favor of investment options they may
have previously ignored—in particular mutual funds and annuities. If you are considering these options, bear in mind
that while these investments may pay higher yields than
savings options, they also entail greater risk, are not insured
by deposit insurance, and have costs (and complexities) associated with them that should be factored into your purchase decision. Given this, you need to know what you are
getting yourself into before you put your savings into them.

As you contemplate different investment options, you
should strive to diversify your investments. For example,
you might not want to keep all of your money in insured accounts earning low rates of interest. Conversely, you probably do not want to subject all of your savings to risk by investing everything you have in the stock market. Many
people opt for a balanced approach where they put some of
their money into insured accounts and place other resources
in higher risk/higher yield investments.

Mutual Funds

Many people like to invest in the stock and bond markets, trying to second-guess their ups and downs and hoping that their risk-taking will pay off. Some invest themselves, while others rely upon brokerage firms, financial planners, and others to give them advice. The curse (or the blessing) in individual stocks and bonds is that the value of your investment precisely parallels the fluctuations in the value of the stock or bond; if it takes a nosedive (or goes through the roof), your investment does so as well. What's more, investing in the stock or bond market is a fairly labor-intensive endeavor. You either need to keep abreast of the latest developments yourself or confer regularly with a professional concerning your investment decisions.

If you lack the temperament, fortitude, or time necessary for successful stock or bond market investment, you might consider investing in mutual funds. These funds, which may allow you to reap higher returns than CDs, provide a simple, low-cost way to participate in the financial markets. They pool the money of many investors through the purchase of a variety of stocks, bonds, and other securities. Given this feature, your investment is not linked to the performance of any particular security. Instead, mutual fund performance is based upon the performance of *the combination* of securities in the mutual fund portfolio. This diversification is designed to insulate you from significant harm in the event any one stock or bond or a number of stocks and bonds in the portfolio do not do well. Barring a major market downturn where all securities lose value, losses in one part of the portfolio are often offset by gains in another. This will minimize the risk of investing in the various financial markets.

Mutual funds are managed by investment professionals who select the funds included in the portfolio. As a result, you are spared having to keep up with market fluctuations or having to make ongoing investment decisions (like which securities to hold, when to buy, or when to sell).

When you invest in a mutual fund, you are buying shares in it. Your share ownership is proportional to the amount you invest. You, and the other people who invest in the fund, are co-owners of the fund. When the fund makes money, earnings are distributed either as dividends or as capital gains. If you so choose, most funds will allow you to reinvest dividends and capital gains through the purchase of additional shares, thus increasing your ownership share.

Unlike term deposits such as CDs where your funds are committed for a definite period of time, you are free to cash in all or part of your shares at any time. Mutual funds, therefore, represent liquid assets that give you the flexibility of redeeming your shares at their net asset value (the market value of all securities in the fund's portfolio, divided by the number of shares outstanding) whenever you wish. You also do not have to find a buyer for your shares. The mutual fund company stands ready to buy back any shares you may have purchased. What's more, if you invest in a "family" of funds (where several funds are available through one mutual fund company), you are usually free to transfer your money among the different funds within the family. You must be careful doing this, however, since selling shares in a fund, even though you use the proceeds to buy into another fund, can result in a taxable gain (or loss) to you.

The biggest difference between bank and mutual fund accounts is that mutual fund accounts are not FDIC-insured, regardless of whether you bought them through your bank. In addition, most observers recommend that mutual funds be used as long-term investments. So if you're hoping to make a fast buck, mutual funds may not be the appropriate investment vehicle for you.

Federal law requires that you be provided with a copy of the mutual fund prospectus before you invest in a fund. This prospectus provides you with all of the pertinent information you need to know about the fund when making an investment decision. It is well worth your while to carefully review the prospectuses of any mutual funds in which you may be interested. Since there are over 3,800 mutual funds on the market, you will need to compare different products and select a mutual fund that best meets your investment needs. Mutual fund sales are regulated by the U.S. Securities and Exchange Commission.

❑ Types of Mutual Funds
There are two basic types of mutual funds.

Closed-End Funds. Only a limited number of shares are available in closed-end mutual funds. After the initial shares are sold, no further investments into these funds are accepted. The fund is closed to keep it from becoming unmanageable and unwieldy. Shares of a closed-end fund are traded like stocks. Typically, these funds sell at a discount from net asset value, although a few such funds often sell at premiums over net asset value. Closed-end funds are especially attractive when they are selling at large discounts. People normally find out about the availability of closed-end funds through tips from stockbrokers, financial planners, and other such professionals. Before buying, be sure you know what the typical discount is.

Open-End Funds. Additional shares of these funds are issued on a continuous basis, with the proceeds going into the fund's investment portfolio. Occasionally, open-end funds will temporarily be closed to new investors. Most funds are open-end funds.

❏ Other Fund Distinctions

Index Funds. Index funds invest in a wide range of securities. Portfolios are constructed to mirror movements in a broad stock or bond market index, like the Standard & Poor's 500 Stock Index or the Shearson Lehman Bond Index. Index funds, therefore, are designed to do about as well as the stock and bond markets in general. An index fund will include stocks and bonds that are industry leaders or whose performance is in keeping with market performance. An index fund will not protect you, however, if the stock or bond market as a whole declines substantially.

Specialty Funds. Specialty funds invest in certain geographic areas or industries. For example, a medical specialty fund would invest in health-related securities only. Some funds have adopted certain social objectives or follow special investment philosophies.

Stock Funds. Stock funds invest in different types of stocks. Growth funds invest primarily in established companies. Aggressive growth funds invest in smaller, less proven, more volatile companies.

Bond Funds. Bond funds invest in different types of corporate and/or government bonds. Bond purchasers agree to loan money to the corporate or governmental entity issuing a bond in exchange for the payment of interest. Many of these bonds are high-denomination and would normally be beyond the reach of the ordinary investor. A mutual fund, however, has the financial capability to invest in bonds, thus benefiting its shareholders. A corporate bond fund invests in corporate bonds. Government bond funds invest in U.S. Treasury securities. Tax-free bond funds invest in state or municipal government bonds.

Balanced Funds. While some funds invest solely in stocks or bonds, others use a mixture of stocks and bonds, combining the stability of government securities with the income-producing capabilities of stocks.

Money Market Funds. Money market funds invest in very stable financial instruments (like commercial paper and government Treasuries).These funds are generally not subjected to fluctuations in the stock or bond market. For more information on money market funds, consult chapter six.

Before investing in any of these funds, you must first determine the degree of risk you are willing to assume and invest accordingly. With the range of offerings available, you should be able to select a mutual fund with an investment objective that helps you accomplish your own financial goals.

❏ Risk and Return

Within the mutual fund field, you can select options that minimize your risk while giving you a modest rate of return or that assume a great deal of risk and hold forth the prospect of great returns. The types of funds, and their relative risks and returns, are indicated below.

AGGRESSIVE COMMON STOCK GROWTH FUNDS

Highest Risk/Return

Growth funds

Growth and income funds

Income funds

Balanced funds

Corporate bond funds

Government bond funds

Money market funds

Lowest Risk/Return

❑ Costs

There are a number of costs associated with mutual fund purchases. These may include the following.

Load Funds vs. No-Load Funds. A "load" is nothing more than a commission to sales personnel. "Front end" loads, ranging anywhere from 0.5 to 8.5 percent of your investment, are assessed by some funds when you purchase mutual fund shares. You should avoid paying a load fee by selecting one of the many available no-load funds. If you choose to purchase a front-end load fund, try to keep the load as low as possible (no more than 1 to 2 percent). Other funds may assess a "back end" load, or contingent deferred sales charge. This charge, which may be as high as 6 percent of your original investment, will most likely decline the longer you hold your investment. Still other funds may have hidden loads in the form of "12b-1" fees. These fees, which range from 0.1 to 1.25 percent, are assessed annually to cover fund expenses like marketing, distribution, and advertising. Unlike sales commissions, these fees are charged against fund assets and are not paid directly by the investor.

Many experts agree that there is no significant difference in the performance of load versus no-load mutual funds. Thus, load fees do not improve performance. They do, however, reduce the return you reap on your investment. Given this, try to avoid load funds. The mutual funds sold by banks, stockbrokers, financial planners, and insurance agents are load funds. Load fees are how they make their money on mutual funds.

To purchase no-load mutual funds, you will need to deal directly with a mutual fund company or with a discount brokerage house that offers no-load funds. Spotting a no-load fund is fairly easy. Mutual fund pricing information appears in the business sections of most major newspapers; no-load funds are usually clearly indicated. In addition, no-load funds are highly advertised in many newspapers across the country. Your local library may also be a good source of information. Once there, you might review one of the mutual fund rating services (like Morningstar and Donoghue's) or information developed by the American Association of Individual Investors (AAII). If you find a no-load fund you may be interested in, contact the company for more information.

Redemption Fees. Some funds charge anywhere from 0.5 to 2 percent of the fund's value as a fee for redeeming shares. Since such redemption fees exact a considerable toll on earnings, avoid funds with redemption fees.

Management Fees. Most funds charge annual fees of
0.5 to 1.5 percent for managing your investment. Your
goal, therefore, is to find funds with the lowest possible
management fees. Remember, management fees are in addition to loads or other charges that may be assessed.

Before investing in any mutual fund, carefully analyze
the cumulative impact of the various fees discussed above.
These will all be disclosed in the prospectus. The goal is to
avoid load funds with high management fees and strive toward low- or no-load funds with low management fees.
This will minimize your expenses and maximize the amount
of your investment that is working for you.

❑ Fund Performance

On a mutual fund prospectus you will see charts indicating the fund's performance for various periods of time—one
year, five years, and ten years. These figures give you some
indication of how a particular fund performed in years past,
and how it might perform in the future. Be aware, however,
that a fund's previous performance may not be a good pre-
dictor of its future performance. Instead of using fund performance as your barometer, it is probably better to assess a
fund's risk and return status (discussed earlier) and to make
your decision upon the risk you are willing to assume and
the return you expect.

❑ Selecting a Fund Manager

When shopping for a mutual fund, try to assess the com-
petence of the fund's manager. This holds true for most
types of funds in which you may invest, with the exception
of index funds, where management is less significant. Some
funds are managed by an individual; others are managed by
a team. If a particular manager or team has been controlling

the fund for quite a while, you can easily assess its performance under that management. If a particular fund is part of a mutual fund family, you might also get prospectuses and look into the performance of other funds managed by the same person or group. If you are not entirely comfortable with the fund's management capabilities, consider finding another fund in whose management you have more confidence.

❑ Purchase Methods

You have two basic options when investing in a mutual fund. First, you can buy directly from the mutual fund company of your choice. Since most of these companies have toll-free numbers staffed by trained professionals who are prepared to answer your every question and send you appropriate materials, shopping is fairly easy to accomplish. While this may take a little bit of time and effort on your part, you will reduce your costs by avoiding sales charges. Second, you can rely upon professional advice from a banker, stockbroker, financial planner, or insurance agent who is registered to sell mutual funds. These professionals, however, will charge sales commissions through a load fee attached to your transaction.

Mutual funds can be purchased in different increments. A maturing certificate of deposit or other investment-ready funds can be used to open up a new mutual fund account or contribute to an existing one through a lump-sum deposit. The process is almost the same as opening up a bank account. Some funds have minimum initial deposit requirements ranging from several hundred to several thousand dollars. These requirements are often waived if you are opening up a retirement account or if you authorize automatic payments, as described below. You can also make periodic payments into your mutual fund account whenever you wish simply by mailing in your deposit or accomplishing an electronic transfer (wire, automated teller machine, or automated clearinghouse transfer).

Many mutual funds allow you to make automatic deposits into your mutual fund account. To accomplish this, you have to authorize the mutual fund to withdraw a specified amount of money from your bank account on the same date each month. If you are investing in a no-load fund, this is an ideal way to make small, regular investments without incurring high sales costs. It is also a convenient way of saving, since the money is withdrawn from your bank account before you even realize it is there. With this automatic payment feature, you must make certain to record your mutual fund payments so you will not overdraft your account. This automatic payment feature is normally available whether or not you purchase your mutual fund from your bank.

Annuities

Like mutual funds, annuities are increasingly popular. These financial contracts can be purchased from insurance agents, financial planners, and from more and more banks.

An annuity is an investment contract between you and an insurance company. In exchange for your payment or payments, the company promises to provide you with a stream of income according to the terms of your agreement. You place funds on deposit either in periodic installments or in a lump sum. Payments under an annuity contract, which can begin either immediately upon your deposit or at some future date (upon your retirement, for example), last as long as you live or for a specified period of time.

Annuities are insurance contracts. They are not deposit accounts that qualify for deposit insurance coverage. Should the insurance company fail, you could lose some or all of your money. Before putting your money into an annuity, you should make certain that the insurance company offering it is sound by checking with one of the insurance company rating services (like AM Best or Moody's).

Annuities do not require you to manage investments (this will be done by the insurance company), report interest or dividends, delve into the intimacies of financial markets, or compete against professional investors. The interest rates paid on annuities, which are normally higher than what you can obtain on CDs or other time instruments from banks, are often comparable to long-term bond rates. In addition, some annuities let you borrow against your accumulated contract value; many allow you to use it as collateral for a bank loan.

❑ Types of Annuities
The following identifies different types of features common to annuities.

Immediate annuity. Monthly payments begin immediately after the initial payment has been made.

Deferred annuity. You earn tax-deferred interest on your investment until payments begin at some future date.

Single premium annuity. You make a one-time annuity deposit.

Flexible premium annuity. You make unlimited periodic deposits into your annuity account.

Variable annuity. Your account's value changes with fluctuations in stock or bond prices.

Fixed annuity. You are guaranteed a certain interest rate on your annuity earnings.

If you are interested in purchasing an annuity, you should shop around for the best deals possible. Compare different products from different providers. Pricing characteristics vary considerably; tremendous variations in payouts, fees, and interest earnings exist. In such an environment, you need to do your homework before investing.

❑ **Tax Benefit**
One of the primary benefits of deferred annuities is their tax-deferred status. Since annual annuity earnings are not considered taxable income, they accumulate in your annuity account tax-free until you withdraw them. For most people, withdrawal occurs during retirement, when they will likely be in a lower tax bracket. What's more, you can still invest any amount you wish in an annuity and reap tax-deferred earnings even though you have made maximum IRA and pension contributions for the year.

❑ **Costs and Minimums**
Be on the lookout for different types of charges and fees that can have a significant impact upon your overall earnings. Pricing characteristics include the following:

No-load plans: no sales charges are levied.

Front-end loads: commissions to sales personnel (usually from 3 to 8 percent).

Maintenance fees: annual fees for maintaining your account usually around $30).

Asset management fees: similar to mutual fund operating expenses (range from 0.3 to 2.5 percent of your investment annually).

Insurance expenses: covers mortality and expense risk (about 1.25 percent annually).

Surrender fees: penalties for withdrawing more than 10 percent of your contract value ahead of schedule (about 15 percent in the first year, 1 percent less thereafter, until unearned expenses of insurance company have been recouped).

Some annuities, like a single-premium deferred annuity, may require a minimum initial deposit of $2,500 to $10,000. Flexible premium annuities, on the other hand, may accept periodic payments of less than $100.

While annuities, because they are tax-free, may be good investments for some, they tend to be more costly than mutual funds. Many people are able to reap similarly tax-free earnings by funding an individual retirement account through a no-load mutual fund (up to $2,000 a year for an individual). So unless you plan to stick with an annuity for the long haul, you might be better off investing in a no-load mutual fund instead.

R E C O M M E N D A T I O N S

If you are considering investing in a mutual fund or an annuity, understand that neither is insured by the FDIC. As uninsured products, you are exposed to risks that are not associated with insured deposit accounts.

Mutual funds and annuities are appropriate investment options for some people. There are costs associated with each, however, that must be factored into your investment decision. A plethora of products is available from which to choose. Given this, you probably need to learn more about these different products and check out different providers to see where you can get the best bargain.

8

Borrowing Money

Peggy is applying for a loan and wants to reduce her monthly payments by getting the longest length loan possible. While she is focusing upon the monthly payment amount, she simply cannot ignore the total cost of the loan. Since unduly stretching out her monthly payments will substantially increase the cost of her loan, if she can make higher monthly payments, she should apply for the shortest term loan she can afford.

Liz is tempted to borrow money to tie up some loose ends: paint the house, repave the driveway, repair the car, and buy her parents a nice anniversary gift. Taking out a personal, unsecured loan and financing these items will increase their costs. As a result, it may not be in Liz's best interest to borrow money to accomplish these tasks.

Credit serves a variety of needs in our lives. One of its primary purposes is to allow us to "buy now and pay later." By using credit, we gain immediate access to goods and services and are able to enjoy our purchases while we pay for them. It allows us to pay a loan off over time. Credit also enables us to purchase expensive items that we would normally have difficulty paying for outright.

When to Borrow

Before deciding whether to borrow money, ask yourself the following three questions: Do I need credit? Can I afford credit? Can I qualify for credit?

❑ Do I Need Credit?

Many people borrow money when they really do not need to or cannot afford it. Loans are expensive and can substantially increase the cost of items financed. So before signing on the dotted line, consider paying with cash. If you cannot afford to pay cash for smaller items, you probably cannot afford them through credit usage either. It is a good idea to try forgoing a purchase entirely or delaying it until you are better able to afford it. You could even develop a savings strategy for making an upcoming purchase. By doing this, you save money and give yourself time to think the purchase through. Who knows, maybe it will go on sale while you are saving; perhaps you will find something you like better at a lower price. While you may not be able to save up enough to finance the entire purchase, at the very least try to make a substantial downpayment. With a smaller loan amount and a shorter loan period, you will be able to decrease your costs considerably.

Easy access to installment loans often encourages people to make expensive purchases they may later regret. With "easy payment plans" and "instantaneous credit" so readily available, you really need to stop and think before committing yourself. Sometimes you will be confronted with hard-sell marketing techniques (for example, when shopping on the last day of a "summer blowout") or the salesperson may be pressuring you to take the leap. Do not be pressured into making a hasty decision. Take a deep breath and walk away for a little while (an hour or so, maybe even a day or two). You need time to mull over what you are getting yourself into and to calculate how much this item will ultimately cost you. Think things over carefully. Unless the store is going out of business, the chances are pretty good that you will still be able to get the benefit of the bargain.

If you have available savings, you might consider dipping into it instead of financing your purchase through a loan. For example, suppose you have a savings account that is earning 3.5 percent interest and you have sufficient funds on deposit in this account to finance your proposed purchase. If you take out a 16 percent loan, there is a 12.5 percent gap between what you are earning on your savings versus what you will pay on your loan. Your lost interest earnings will pale in comparison to the amount of money you would have lost through loan payments at the higher rate.

Should you decide to use savings, view the transaction as a loan to yourself. Develop a definite monthly repayment plan. Make payments back to your savings just as you would with an ordinary loan. Instead of using all of your savings, you might also consider setting aside a small portion so you will be prepared for the unexpected. Do not let dipping into your savings discourage future savings.

❑ Can I Afford Credit?

Before borrowing, ask whether you can meet all essential expenses and still afford monthly loan payments. You can determine this in one of three ways. First, do you currently save enough of your take-home pay to afford the monthly payments? If you do not, it will probably be difficult to forgo other purchases in order to make the payments. Are you prepared to give up spending on clothing, entertainment, or eating out in order to afford the new car or home improvements you wish to finance?

Second, add up all basic monthly expenses and compare this total with your take-home pay. If the difference would not cover a monthly payment and still leave funds for discretionary and incidental expenses, you cannot afford the loan. For example, assume a family with $2,000 in monthly take-home pay and other income has monthly expenses for food, rent, utilities, and insurance totaling approximately $1,500. There is no way this family can afford $350 monthly payments and still cover other expenses. When assessing your budget situation, do not cut yourself too close. Everyone needs flexibility in his or her budget; money must be available for discretionary and unanticipated spending needs.

Third, does your existing outstanding indebtedness plus the amount of the proposed new loan fall within acceptable guidelines? Most knowledgeable observers agree that your installment debts (including your outstanding car loans, personal loans, student loans, credit cards, lines of credit, but excluding your mortgage) should not exceed more than 15 to 20 percent of your annual take-home pay. Remember, this is take-home, net pay; not gross earnings. If you have more than this percentage in outstanding debt, you are overextended and may even be in or precariously close to credit difficulties.

Given this, it is important to calculate your total indebtedness and determine what percentage of your annual take-home pay this represents. Make sure to include all types of indebtedness (including the new loan you are considering) as you do your calculation. List each creditor along with your current outstanding balance in the spaces provided below. Then total these figures.

HOW MUCH DO YOU CURRENTLY OWE?

Creditor	Outstanding Balance
_____	$_____
_____	$_____
_____	$_____
_____	$_____
_____	$_____
_____	$_____
_____	$_____
_____	$_____
_____	$_____
(Potential New Creditor)	(Amount)

Total Indebtedness $_____

Once you have determined your total indebtedness, compare this figure to the reasonable debt loads reflected below for different take-home-pay levels.

If the addition of this new loan amount would throw your indebtedness above 20 percent of your annual take-home pay, you should seriously reconsider taking on this new obligation. What's more, if you are already above the 20 percent threshold without the new loan, you need to take steps immediately to reduce rather than increase your indebtedness.

RECOMMENDED INCOME-TO-DEBT RATIOS

Take-Home Pay		Debt Levels	
Per Month	Per Year	15 %	20 %
$ 250	$3,000	$450	$600
$ 500	$6,000	$900	$1,200
$ 750	$9,000	$1,350	$1,800
$1,000	$12,000	$1,800	$2,400
$1,250	$15,000	$2,250	$3,000
$1,500	$18,000	$2,700	$3,600
$1,750	$21,000	$3,150	$4,200
$2,000	$24,000	$3,600	$4,800
$2,250	$27,000	$4,050	$5,400
$2,500	$30,000	$4,500	$6,000
$2,750	$33,000	$4,950	$6,600
$3,000	$36,000	$5,400	$7,200
$3,250	$39,000	$5,850	$7,800
$3,500	$42,000	$6,300	$8,400
$3,750	$45,000	$6,750	$9,000

To make absolutely certain you can afford a loan, you need a ballpark estimate of expected loan payments. Using the table below, find the applicable interest rate, look across at the monthly payments required for the various time periods, and multiply by the multiple of 1,000 that represents the total amount of your loan.

PAYMENTS ON A $1,000 LOAN

Interest Rate(%)	12 Mos.	24 Mos.	36 Mos.	48 Mos.	60 Mos.
0	$83.33	$41.67	$27.78	$20.83	$16.67
1	$83.79	$42.12	$28.23	$21.28	$17.12
2	$84.25	$42.57	$28.68	$21.73	$17.57
3	$84.71	$43.02	$29.13	$22.18	$18.03

Interest Rate(%)	12 Mos.	24 Mos.	36 Mos.	48 Mos.	60 Mos.
4	$85.17	$43.47	$29.58	$22.63	$18.49
5	$85.63	$43.92	$30.03	$23.08	$18.95
6	$86.09	$44.37	$30.48	$23.54	$19.41
7	$86.55	$44.82	$30.93	$24.00	$19.87
8	$87.01	$45.27	$31.38	$24.46	$20.33
9	$87.47	$45.72	$31.83	$24.92	$20.79
10	$87.92	$46.15	$32.27	$25.37	$21.25
11	$88.39	$46.41	$32.74	$25.85	$21.75
12	$88.85	$47.08	$33.22	$26.34	$22.25
13	$89.32	$47.55	$33.70	$26.83	$22.76
14	$89.79	$48.02	$34.18	$27.33	$23.27
15	$90.26	$48.49	$34.67	$27.84	$23.79
16	$90.74	$48.97	$35.16	$28.35	$24.32
17	$91.21	$49.45	$35.66	$28.86	$24.86
18	$91.68	$49.93	$36.16	$29.38	$25.40
19	$92.15	$50.41	$36.66	$29.90	$25.94
20	$92.62	$50.89	$37.16	$30.42	$26.48
21	$93.09	$51.37	$37.66	$30.92	$27.02

❑ Can I Qualify for Credit?

Be Aware of Credit Overextension Thresholds. You should understand that most creditors will not loan you money if you already have 20 percent or more of your annual take-home pay in outstanding consumer debt (excluding your mortgage). If you have debt levels in excess of this 20 percent threshold, you are overextended, and few creditors will allow you to further increase your debt burden. If they did, they might not be able to get their money back. So if your current indebtedness is in excess of 20 percent of your annual take-home pay, you will probably need to pay down your outstanding balances before applying for a new loan. You do not want to go to all the trouble of getting your hopes up and filling out an application if it is a foregone conclusion that you will not qualify. Similarly, if you are considering applying for a new loan at some point in the future, plan ahead by reducing your indebtedness accordingly so your application will be viewed as favorably as possible by prospective creditors.

Credit-granting System. Here is how the credit-granting system works. You fill out an application which the creditor reviews. At the same time, a copy of your credit report will be obtained from a credit-reporting agency (also known as a credit bureau). Then your prospective creditor will determine if you are a good credit risk and whether they will loan you money. They do this by scoring you on the basis of several factors, including the "three Cs":

Capacity—Can you repay the debt?

Character—Will you repay the debt?

Collateral—Is the creditor protected if you fail to repay?

Today, the credit-granting process is highly automated and utilizes computerized credit-scoring systems. Through these systems, creditors look for stability through indicators that reflect that you are responsible in your affairs: your past credit activities, your current indebtedness to other creditors, your current income and length of employment, whether you can afford to make the required loan payments, whether you own a home, how long you have lived at your current address, your assets, the security pledged (can the creditor easily regain possession of your purchase in the event you default on your loan?), etc. Once this information has been reviewed, a creditor will rate you. Depending upon your rating, your credit application will either be accepted or rejected.

Each creditor is free to use its own credit-scoring system based upon its experiences in granting credit to others. These systems can include whichever factors a creditor deems important. However, the federal Equal Credit Opportunity Act (ECOA) prohibits creditors from discriminating against you on the basis of race, sex, marital status, national origin, religion, age, or because you receive public assistance. Given the fact that credit-scoring systems vary considerably, it is entirely possible for one creditor to accept and another to deny your application based upon identical information.

If your application is rejected, the creditor must notify you in writing within thirty days of receipt of your application, either explaining the specific reasons for this refusal or indicating your right to an explanation. In addition, if a credit report was used when making a determination on your application, the identity of the credit-reporting agency must also be disclosed.

Special Credit Problems. You may encounter special problems if you are new to the credit market. Suppose you just graduated from college or have never borrowed money before. Because you do not have a credit-history on file with the credit-reporting agencies, your creditor has no independent means of assessing your creditworthiness. As a result, you may find yourself at a severe disadvantage in obtaining your first loan. To establish a strong financial identity, you may need to open a small account. Try a local department store where you often shop, or check out credit offerings of organizations to which you belong (labor unions, professional organizations, etc.). You might establish a savings account at a local financial institution, then borrow against these funds. If you have an existing relationship with a financial institution, you may be able to parlay this into a freestanding loan. Or you might consider asking someone who is financially responsible to cosign a loan for you. Once you get a loan, be diligent in your repayment activities. This should establish a strong financial identity for you upon which prospective lenders can base future lending decisions.

Similarly, it is very important for women in relationships to develop their own financial identities separate and apart from their spouses or partners. Many women neglect this important part of their lives. Some wind up paying a considerable price should their husband or loved one die, become incapacitated, or if divorce or separation occurs. To protect themselves, women need to apply for credit in their own names or participate in joint accounts. Both of these actions will help them develop a strong financial identity on which they can rely.

Where to Borrow

When most people think about loans, they naturally think about borrowing money from financial institutions (banks, savings and loans, and credit unions). If a loan is in the offing for you, consider the various options identified below and respond accordingly.

❏ Deposited Funds
Some financial institutions are willing to lend you money against funds you have on deposit at their institution. For example, if you have a CD or other savings at a particular institution, you might take out a loan using your deposited

funds as collateral. Under such circumstances, financial institutions may be willing to lend you money at fairly low rates. Borrowing against this bank-held collateral may be the cheapest way to borrow from an institution with which you already have a relationship. So while it may not be practical to cash in your CDs to finance a purchase (because of early-withdrawal penalties, for example), you may still be able to utilize them as collateral for a loan.

❏ **Relatives, Close Friends, or Business Associates**
     A relative, close friend, or business associate may prove to be a convenient loan source. Such a credit extension can be very helpful, particularly since such loans are often offered on very favorable terms. In many cases, these loans are extended with no expectation of interest or with an interest rate that approximates what your benefactor would have earned on the money through savings.
     Before borrowing money from relatives, friends, or business associates, understand that financial entanglements can quickly strain relationships. Therefore, it is important to set out the terms of the agreement in writing before any money ever changes hands. Both parties must be totally aware of all rights and responsibilities. A basic promissory note should be entered into that will protect the interests of both parties and circumvent any potential misunderstandings about the terms of the agreement.

❏ **Life Insurance Companies**
     Most consumers with whole-life insurance policies can borrow on the accumulated cash value of the policy at a guaranteed rate. This rate is often less than rates charged by financial institutions. However, keep in mind that borrowing this cash value reduces your insurance policy's financial

protection unless you purchase term insurance to make up the difference. Term insurance, however, is usually available only to those with policies that pay dividends ("participating" policies). Some insurance companies also now offer "living benefits" policies which allow you to access a portion of the proceeds from your life insurance policy while you are still alive. These policies are normally only available to people with life-threatening illnesses. If you are considering borrowing against an insurance policy, discuss the possibilities with your insurance agent to determine which options might be best for you.

❑ Banks and Savings and Loans

Financial institutions (banks, savings and loans, and credit unions) often offer a full range of loan products. In many instances, financial institution loans carry some of the most reasonably priced interest rates around. This is particularly true if you are interested in a home equity loan or a personal, unsecured loan. Rates on these types of loans tend to be lower than those offered by the same institution on other products (for example, a personal, unsecured loan may go for 14—16 percent, while credit cards are in the 17—20 percent range). Given this, you might consider one of these loans as a way of paying off your high-interest-rate credit cards.

On other types of loans (for example, new-car loans), however, the interest rates charged by financial institutions may be higher than what you can obtain through other sources (for example, dealer financing). For example, you may be able to get 4.9 percent dealer financing on a new-car loan, while a bank's most attractive rate is only 8.9 percent. So your best bet is to shop around and compare different provider offerings to find your best deal.

❑ Credit Unions

Credit unions are nonprofit organizations that provide services only to people who qualify under their "common bond." This common bond arises through a variety of circumstances—employment, membership in religious, fraternal, community, and civic groups, membership in employment-related organizations (like labor unions, state teachers' associations, or state bar associations), and other affiliations. For example, the Navy Federal Credit Union's services can only be offered to Navy personnel who join the credit union. An outsider who is not employed by the Navy cannot join. However, if you open an account with a credit union while you qualify for membership, you can still maintain this account even though you may later find employment elsewhere. Because credit union services are offered to members, credit unions often charge fairly low interest rates on the money they lend as well as pay higher interest rates on money members invest with them.

❑ Finance Companies

Finance companies often lend to those who cannot obtain credit from other lenders. The problem with most finance companies is finding one that offers loans on reasonable terms and does not charge you a high interest rate. While most financial institution loans hover a few points above the prime lending rate (the lowest lending rate they give to their best customers), many finance companies charge 21 percent and sometimes upwards of 30 percent for unsecured loans. This is because finance companies often cater to high-risk individuals who cannot get credit elsewhere. So if you are denied credit by a bank, savings and loan, or credit union, you should question your ability to afford the higher rate of a finance company. Only in the most dire of circumstances should you undertake a high-interest-rate loan. But if this is your only option, make every effort to repay it as soon as possible.

❑ Automobile Finance Companies

The only finance companies that usually charge lower loan rates than some financial institutions are those affiliated with major automobile manufacturers (for example, General Motors Acceptance Corporation, Ford Motor Credit, and other similarly situated companies). In an effort to move cars off of salesroom floors, these lenders frequently offer very low rates on certain car models. Many of these are promotional rates which are limited time offerings. Keep in mind that a car dealer offering you such a rate may be less willing to discount the price of the car or throw in free options. A dealer's willingness to "sweeten the deal" may cost you more than any savings from the lower interest rates. To avoid this, negotiate a purchase price before informing the dealer you need financing.

❑ Retailers

A few retailers write and carry their own installment loans, which should be distinguished from the store charge cards they may also offer. Typically, these merchants are used-car lots or furniture and appliance stores selling to moderate-income families. Loans are often offered in order to build customer relationships, sell additional merchandise, and enhance profits by financing products sold. Retail loan rates, which are usually quite high, are often comparable to finance company offerings. As a result, loans from retailers should normally be avoided.

Sample Promissory Note

Date: _____

City: _____

State: _____

I, _____, _____,
    (full name of debtor)   (address, city, state, zip code)

_____, _____,
    (telephone number)   (Social Security number)

_____, do hereby acknowledge the receipt of a cash loan from
(date of birth)

_____, in the amount of _____,
(full name of creditor)   (amount of loan)

made on _____. The purpose of this loan is:_____
    (date of loan)

_____.

I promise to pay to the order of _____,
                  (full name of creditor)

_____, _____,
(address, city, state, zip code)   (telephone number)

the sum of _____, in _____
      (amount of loan)   (number of installments)

of _____ each, with a final payment of _____
  (amount of payment)   (amount of final payment)

on _____. Interest shall be payable at the rate of
    (date)

_____ percent simple interest. Payment shall be due on the
_____ day of each month beginning on _____.
                       (date payments begin)

Any payment not received by the _____ day of the month in which it is due shall be considered in default. As a result of the default of any payment due under this note, _____, or any holder of

(name of creditor)

this note, may declare the entire note due and demand immediate payment in full of the outstanding balance of the note.

Further, interest shall accrue at the rate of _____ % simple interest on the unpaid balance from the date of such demand until payment in full. Any holder of this note shall be entitled to collection costs, court costs, and reasonable attorney's fees.

_____

(full signature of debtor)

_____

(date signed)

How to Borrow

❏ Importance of Low Interest and Short Loans

Consumers will often agonize over the required monthly payments in an effort to make sure they can afford a new loan. This is laudable, since all consumers should carefully analyze a prospective loan's impact upon their budgets. Where most people make mistakes, however, is in paying too much attention to the monthly payment and too little attention to a loan's annual percentage rate (APR) and its length. As discussed earlier, the interest rate has a significant impact upon your loan's cost. Given this, try to keep the APR as low as possible. Similarly, be careful not to unduly stretch out your loan payments over a long time period in order to bring down your monthly payments. Again, this will cost you more in the long run. Getting the best available interest rate and the shortest loan repayment period you can afford will save you lots of money.

It is very important to compute the ultimate cost of your loan. A $5,000 loan would yield the following monthly payments and total costs at three different interest rates during the indicated loan periods.

$5,000 LOAN MONTHLY PAYMENTS AND TOTAL COSTS

Loan Length	Monthly Payments (Total Loan Cost)		
	10 %	15 %	20 %
1 year	$439.60 ($5,275.20)	$451.30 ($5,415.60)	$463.10 ($5,557.20)
2 years	$230.75 ($5,538.00)	$242.45 ($5,818.80)	$254.45 ($6,106.80)
3 years	$161.35 ($5,808.60)	$173.35 ($6,240.60)	$185.80 ($6,688.80)
4 years	$126.50 ($6,072.00)	$139.20 ($6,681.60)	$152.10 ($7,300.80)
5 years	$106.25 ($6,375.00)	$118.95 ($7,137.00)	$132.40 ($7,944.00)

This table graphically demonstrates the cost of credit. You can really see the impact of the interest rate on the amount financed over time. For example, on a five-year loan, the total interest paid at 10 percent is $1,375. It is almost mind-boggling to think that the total interest paid at 20 percent is $2,944. Thus, at 10 percent, you shave ten percentage points off the loan and also save $1,569. Obviously, the lower the interest rate, the cheaper the loan.

As the table also shows, the length of the repayment period also substantially affects a loan's ultimate costs. With a five-year loan at 15 percent interest, you wind up paying a whopping $2,137 in interest costs over the course of the loan. If you could repay the loan in three years instead of five (still at 15 percent), you would pay $1,240.60 and save yourself $896.40. If you winnowed the length of the loan down to one year, you would pay $415.60 in interest and

save $1,721.40 over the five-year loan. Thus, if you can af-
ford a shorter repayment period, you will save money.

Be aware of the longer term consequences of getting
into debt. You probably have lots of dreams and needs for
the future. To accomplish these, you do not want to be
saddled with long-term debt because of a purchase decision
you make today. You need to think these long-term reper-
cussions through before committing yourself.

❑ Charges That Can Increase the Cost of Credit

Credit Insurance. Millions of American consumers are
falling prey to a big rip-off—credit insurance. Many lenders
offer various forms of credit life and disability insurance attached to their loans. In the event of your death, credit life
insurance will pay your outstanding loan balance in full, thus
protecting your family from having to pay the remainder of
your loan. Credit disability insurance (also known as acci-
dent and health insurance) covers your payments if your
principal income is cut off because of illness or disability.
Once you recover, your obligation to repay resumes. There
is considerable variation in charges assessed for different
types of credit insurance, with premiums on each policy
ranging from a hundred to several hundred dollars. These
premiums, which are based upon your loan amount, obviously increase significantly as the loan size grows. Since
policy costs are included as part of your financed loan
amount, you wind up paying interest on them. This further
increases your ultimate cost.

Consumers often report that they buy credit insurance
for one of two reasons: because they thought it was required or because they thought it might enhance their
chances for loan approval. Neither of these assumptions is

correct. Credit insurance is not required for you to qualify for a loan. No local, state, or federal law requires you to purchase credit insurance. As a result, lenders cannot legally require you to purchase credit insurance with a loan. That said, many lenders will do everything they can to try to pressure you into buying it, because the sale of credit insurance further increases their profit on your loan.

In addition, lending decisions are not based upon whether you purchase credit insurance. To the contrary, these are based upon the host of other unrelated factors described earlier in this chapter. Unfortunately, you are often asked to decide whether you wish to purchase credit insurance as part of the loan application process. Although included as part of this process, your decisions on credit insurance will not in any way influence whether your loan is approved or rejected. Your application will stand or fall on its own merits.

Credit life and disability insurance policies are some of the most costly forms of insurance on the market today. Their payout ratios are much lower than most other types of insurance. This is because very few consumers actually qualify for benefits by dying or becoming disabled over the course of their loans. Even if these events occur, the indebtedness may have already been considerably reduced through repayment activities. Thus, consumers often pay through the nose for products that yield them little or no value. What's more, many families do not even need this insurance protection. In the event of death or disability, many people can resort to other payment sources—life or disability insurance proceeds, workers' compensation, savings accounts, or other liquid assets.

If you are like most people, you probably should not waste your money on credit insurance policies you probably do not even need. That said, these high-cost policies can be appropriate under limited circumstances for those people who do not have other insurance coverage, or lack adequate savings or other funding sources on which they can rely. However, if you are going to take out credit insurance, you need to be aware of what you are getting yourself into before you put an "x" in the credit insurance box on the loan application.

Prepayment Penalties. Some financial institutions assess prepayment penalties on selected loans. These charges, which penalize borrowers who repay a loan prior to its scheduled pay-off date, range anywhere from $10 to $50. Prepayment penalties assure the creditor an adequate rate of return on their extension of credit to you. By paying a loan off early, you are saving the amount of money you would have paid in interest during the remainder of the loan. Your creditor will make less profit on the loan because of this. Since prepayment penalties cannot be assessed unless they are specifically called for in the credit agreement or note evidencing the debt, check your loan documents before paying off a loan ahead of schedule. If a prepayment penalty will be assessed, call your institution to see if it will enforce this contractual provision. Some do; others do not. If a penalty will be charged, evaluate whether the money you save through prepayment is more than the penalty you pay.

Late-Payment Fees. Many financial services providers assess penalties for making late payments. They add on late charges when they receive a payment after its due date or after a certain period of time after the due date. Policies governing when late-payment fees are assessed vary among

creditors and the charges vary considerably. Some lenders
base their late fee upon a percentage (normally 5 to 10 percent) of your payment due. Others will charge a set dollar
amount ($5 to $20). These charges are assessed each month
in which a late payment is received. If this occurs on more
than one occasion, the charges can quickly mount up.

Service Charges. Many financial services providers assess other types of service charges. On secured loans, you
may be charged an "acquisition fee" for the lender to acquire an interest in the security pledged. Some lenders assess "processing" or "application" fees of varying sizes,
whether or not your loan application is approved. Sometimes these are refundable; sometimes they are not. Since
these charges can substantially inflate the cost of your loan
and increase your out-of-pocket expenses, their costs
should be factored into your purchase decision. You must
understand that these fees will be imposed on top of the interest rate charged. They are not included as part of your
loan's annual percentage rate (APR).

❑ Practical Considerations
You should shop around for the cheapest loan. This can
be done by calling several lenders to ask about rates. Make
sure you tell the lender the size of the loan, the amount of
the down payment, the length of the loan, and its purpose.
The best indicator of price is not the monthly payment, but
the APR, which takes into consideration all interest and
most other charges (but excludes some service charges, like
late-payment penalties).

Do not be afraid to "haggle." Some lenders are willing
to charge you less than the quoted rate if you negotiate with

them. If you can find a better rate elsewhere, do not hesitate
to mention this fact to another lender. See if they will meet
or beat your best offer.

Also keep in mind that many financial institutions now
offer discounts to borrowers with other account relationships at their institution. So if you have a credit card, checking account, savings account, or do other business with an
institution, you may qualify for a lower loan rate. Similarly,
if you maintain an account and preauthorize monthly payments from it, your loan rate might be reduced by anywhere
from 0.25 to 1 percent.

Your obligation will be bound by the fine print in your
contract. So read your loan documents carefully. If you do
not understand the loan agreement, ask the loan officer to
explain it to you. Or have a lawyer review it. Understand,
however, that if questions or problems arise, you are bound
by what is in your agreement, not by statements made by
bank personnel when you were signing your loan papers.

After getting a new loan, many people make a common
mistake: They view loan proceeds as extra income. This
money is not income; you are borrowing money So do not
spend your loan money on just anything. Earmark it for specific purposes and do not use it to meet ordinary expenses
that should come out of your paycheck. And do not blow
the family budget just because you have gotten a new loan.
While a loan may help to make your life a little easier, it
should never be viewed as a windfall. You need to be very
circumspect in the way you spend this borrowed money.

For many people, it is a good idea not to undertake any
new credit liability until a loan has been repaid in full or, at
the least, substantially paid down. For example, if you take
out a personal, unsecured loan to pay off high-interest-rate

credit cards, do not run these cards back up before you pay off your loan. This will frustrate your purpose in applying for the loan in the first place. You will not only have the loan to repay but your new credit card debts as well. You do not want to build a pyramid of debt that may later collapse on you.

RECOMMENDATIONS

Before deciding to take out a loan, consider paying with cash, even if you must defer the purchase or use existing savings. Make absolutely certain that you can afford credit before applying for a loan. If it is necessary to borrow, explore the possibility of borrowing against funds you may have on deposit; from relatives, close friends, or business associates; against life insurance policies; from banks, savings and loans, and credit unions; and from automobile finance companies. Avoid borrowing from retailers or finance companies at high interest rates. Be sure to factor the cost of credit into your purchase decisions. Understand the importance of low interest rates and short loan lengths and how other charges (like credit insurance, prepayment penalties, late-payment fees, and service charges) can increase a loan's cost.

9

Credit Cards and Other Charge Cards

Don is like many Americans; he never pays his credit card balance in full. The card he uses does not have an annual fee but charges a whopping 19.8 percent interest rate. Although he is fastidious in making at least the minimum payment due each month, he is wasting his money by using a high interest rate card. Since he carries a balance over from month to month, he could easily save hundreds of dollars a year by switching to a lower rate card.

Jo, who has a premium credit card with a $50 annual fee and no grace period, pays her outstanding balance in full each and every month. Because her card does not have a grace period, interest costs start to accrue on the date transactions are posted to her

account. She could save the cost of the annual fee and
stop paying interest on her purchases simply by
switching to a credit card that does not charge an an-
nual fee and has a grace period.

While many kinds of credit products exist, none is more
prevalent than credit cards. They are convenient, safer than
cash, provide leverage in payment disputes, and are easier to
carry and more readily accepted than checks (particularly if
you are away from home). They also offer flexibility by en-
abling you to respond on the spot to life's circumstances,
whether to obtain cash advances or to purchase goods and
services. Credit cards have become indispensable in our
day-to-day functioning. Without one it is difficult, if not impossible, to rent a car, make hotel reservations, or book an
airline ticket. They have also become necessary identification for many daily activities, like cashing a check.

Problems with Plastic

Credit cards are designed to entice us to finance our activities. We are deluged with marketing campaigns that encourage us to "Master the Possibilities" and admonish that
we "Don't Leave Home Without It." We are told "It's
Everywhere You Want to Be" and have learned that "It
Pays to Discover the Card That Pays You Back." These
slick advertising campaigns are so pervasive that they have
crept into the American psyche. In fact, some people are
probably far more likely to know which card is accepted at
Doyle's on the Bay in Sydney Harbor than who represents
them in the United States Congress.

These aggressive marketing campaigns have turned credit cards into "cash cows" for the nation's financial institutions. Indeed, for several years running credit cards have been the most profitable product offered by financial institutions. While in recent years the interest rates paid on savings have been very low (check out CD rates of around 3 percent at your local banks), average credit card interest rates have remained very high (18 percent and greater). Thus, financial institutions have been racking up record profits (in excess of $33 billion in 1992 alone), while millions of consumers have been paying through the nose for the privilege of using plastic.

There is nothing inherently wrong with the use of credit cards. The problem is that they are too convenient, too available. It is almost as if a credit card emits a siren song that beckons us to use it, and use it often. We forget the consequences of our credit card usage because bills are not received until several weeks or a month after transactions occur. In such an environment, consumers must exercise good judgment and restraint.

The American public has developed an unhealthy reliance upon credit cards to finance day-to-day spending needs and to live beyond personal means. Plastic is often viewed as a way of financing one's lifestyle rather than as a tool for responding to important events and spending needs.

In recent years, personal bankruptcy filings have gone through the roof and are now at an all-time high. Indeed, close to 1 million personal bankruptcies were declared in 1992 alone; this number increases by some 50,000 people a year. Millions of Americans are in the throes of credit difficulties, while countless others are financially overextended and only a couple of paychecks away from financial disaster. For some, unforeseen circumstances (like a death in the family, illness, divorce, job loss, even home or auto repairs) would quickly throw them into dire financial straits. Still others are losing money by using cards with exceptionally high interest rates. While recent efforts by some consumers to repay their debts are to be applauded, these actions have barely made a dent in the mountain of debt amassed during the "plastic prosperity" of the eighties. Consumers today owe more than 20 percent of their after-tax income in consumer debt, and most of this debt is on credit cards.

Consider the following. In 1992, 110 million Americans held over 1 billion credit cards. The typical cardholder had 9.1 different cards, with an average total card balance of almost $2,400. The average interest rate charged was about 18 percent. The typical cardholder paid a whopping $450 in credit card interest charges alone (not including annual fees and other service charges). More than two-thirds of credit card holders do not pay their balances in full every month. This means that millions of Americans are carrying over significant credit card debt from month to month, usually at high interest rates.

Types of Credit Cards

While the term "credit card" is widely used, four different types of products actually fall into this category: bank cards, charge cards, retail cards, and secured cards. These products differ in many ways, including the type of institution that offers them, their acceptance by merchants, and their ability to be used to finance purchases. What's more, the terms on different cards vary according to where you live and where the card was issued. Since different rules apply to each, it is important to know the differences.

❑ Bank Cards

Bank cards, such as MasterCard, VISA, Discover, and American Express Optima, are offered through financial institutions (banks, savings and loans, and credit unions). Thus, the MasterCard or VISA you obtain from your local bank is a bank card. Similarly, cards offered by AT&T, General Motors, General Electric, and other nonfinancial providers are bank cards, since they are also offered through financial institutions. Bank cards represent extensions of credit from a financial institution which allow you to purchase services and items from third parties (someone other than the firm extending you credit). They allow you to pay the monthly balance either in full or in installments. Many require the payment of an annual fee; others do not. Some give you a grace period which allows you to avoid interest charges and benefit from a short "float" if you pay your balance in full within a certain time period; others do not offer a grace period. Bank cards assess interest on unpaid balances and cash advances.

If you have a bank card, your card agreement is bound by the laws of the state where your bank card company's operations are actually located. For example, if you live in Texas and have a card issued by a bank in Delaware, your agreement is subject to Delaware's laws, not those of Texas. Recent years have witnessed a mass exodus of bank card operations from states that have enacted restrictive credit card pricing legislation designed to protect consumers. In response, most major credit card operations have been relocated to states that allow higher charges (such as Delaware and South Dakota). Operating out of these states, credit card issuers market their products throughout the country.

It is important to remember that MasterCard and VISA are merely brand names for cards issued by individual finan-

cial institutions. They do not issue the bank cards, nor do
they establish the terms and conditions on these cards.
These are set by each institution offering the card, which is
free to establish its own credit limit, billing policy, annual
fee, interest rate, grace period, minimum payment requirements, etc. For this reason, you will find similarities and differences among these products. Since the terms of bank
cards vary considerably by issuer, it is important to compare
a variety of offerings and to select the one best suited to
your needs and spending patterns.

❏ Charge Cards

Charge cards, such as American Express, Diners Club,
and Carte Blanche, represent another type of card. Like
bank cards, they provide credit availability for third-party
purchases. They are distinguished from bank cards, however, by the fact that they require full payment of the
monthly balance due. Given this payment-in-full feature, no
interest charges are assessed. The failure to pay balances
promptly can lead to the imposition of hefty delinquency
charges as well as cancellation of the card. All of these
cards assess annual fees. Pricing components for charge
cards are governed by the law of the state in which you re-
side.

❏ Retail Cards

Yet another type of card is the retail card, which allows
you to finance purchases made directly from the company
providing the credit, such as a department store. The use of
these cards is usually limited to the issuing retailer; they cannot be used anywhere else. Retail cards, which include department store, gasoline, and airline charge cards, allow you
to pay in full or in installments. No annual fee is charged.

However, interest charges are assessed on unpaid balances.

Retail cards carry some of the highest interest rates in the country. The following listing from *Money Magazine*, January 1993, demonstrates this point. (Figures are for prevailing interest rates. Your rate may vary depending upon the state in which you live.)

Dayton Hudson	21.6%
Federated	21.6%
J.C. Penney	21.0%
Macy's	21.6%
May	21.6%
Montgomery Ward	21.6%
Sears	21.0%
Spiegel/Eddie Bauer	22.6%

Since many retail cards charge interest rates in the 20 percent and above range—a lot higher than those imposed on most bank cards—avoid retail cards if you will <u>not</u> pay the balance in full upon receipt of the bill. Most retailers these days accept bank cards, so if you must carry over your balance and be assessed interest charges, by all means charge your purchases on a lower rate bank card.

Retail card agreements are controlled by the state in which you live. This is why the back of your retail charge statement often contains a table showing the applicable interest rates charged in each state.

❏ **Secured Cards**

Secured cards (which often look just like bank cards) provide credit card privileges through an account that serves as security for your purchases on the card. For example, a secured card that allows you to charge up to $500

will also require you to maintain an account balance of at
least $500 on deposit with the creditor that issued it. If you
default, the creditor can use your collateral—the $500
deposit—to cover the purchases you made on the card.

If you cannot qualify for a bank card or another type of
credit card, you might consider applying for a secured card.
These cards, which are usually not offered through banks,
are offered by finance companies. Since secured cards are
marketed mainly to people who cannot get other cards because of bad credit records or overextension, they are sometimes fairly expensive, charging application fees and/or
transaction charges.

❑ Standard vs. Premium Cards

Although basic or "standard" MasterCard, VISA, and
American Express cards are the most popular, these companies also offer "premium" cards which often carry higher
credit limits and other features, such as higher travel-acci-
dent insurance and special services. These premium cards
often carry stricter qualification criteria and generally cost
more. Typically, the annual fee on premium cards is about
twice that of the standard card; on others the costs are considerably more. For example, American Express Card annual fees: Green, $55; Gold, $75; Platinum, $300. So un-
less you avail yourself of the special services these cards
provide, there may be no need for you to pay their higher
cost. While some people may be impressed by the fact that
you plop down a premium card to pay for dinner, is the per-
ception of prestige really worth the price?

In addition, the credit limit on the standard cards, which
can run pretty high (sometimes a couple of thousand dollars), more than adequately meets most people's needs. If
you are a good customer, these lines of credit tend to creep

upward through automatic increases. You may also wish to avoid the temptation of a large credit line, which may be viewed adversely by other potential creditors. Rather than using a high-cost credit card as a substitute for a loan, if you need to borrow a significant amount of money, take out a personal, unsecured loan at a lower rate.

Factors That Influence Credit Card Costs

Although the interest rate is an important credit-card-pricing component, other factors must be taken into account. These include:

- Amount of the annual fee
- Availability of a grace period (a period of time in which you can pay off current charges interest free)
- Balance calculation method
- Minimum payment amount
- Late-payment fee
- Over-the-limit fee

Factors other than cost may also affect your decision. These include:

- Credit limit
- How widely the card is accepted
- Purchase protection, traveler's and buyer's assurance programs
- Credit card registration services
- Twenty-four-hour toll-free customer service representatives

- ○ Overnight emergency card replacement
- ○ Personal check cashing privileges
- ○ Access to money machine networks and traveler's check dispensers
- ○ Rebate, bonus, and discount programs
- ○ Credit toward future purchases (including vehicles and other goods)
- ○ Frequent-flyer mileage credit
- ○ Insurance protection
- ○ Traveler's assistance
- ○ Admissions to clubs
- ○ Access to tickets for special events
- ○ Year-end activities summaries
- ○ Copies of charge receipts
- ○ Worldwide customer service offices

In addition, consider the card issuer's reputation for customer service. For example, does the issuer act as the cardholder's advocate in disputes with merchants? Some issuers, like American Express, Citibank, and AT&T's Universal Card, have developed well-deserved reputations for their customer service. Universal Card's actions even won the 1992 Malcolm Baldrige National Quality Award.

Certain features may or may not be of importance to you. Yet, their attachment to a particular card will be reflected in its cost. For example, many of the airline frequent-flyer cards couple hefty annual fees with high interest rates. Plus, you often have to charge a lot to get enough "points" to qualify for frequent-flyer bonuses. Hence, the price you pay for bonus mileage credit is dear. In the long run, it might be cheaper and easier to shop around for discounted airline fares than to use a higher cost card merely to obtain mileage credit.

❑ **Calculating Your Annual Credit Card Costs**

The following exercise should help you better understand your annual credit card costs. Since its purpose is to enable you to assess your total credit card expenditures, make certain to include all types of credit cards you may use—bank, charge, and retail cards. First, pull out your most recent January, February, or March bills. One of these will give you the total interest you paid during the preceding year on that particular credit card. Write down in the indicated spaces the appropriate interest figure for every credit card on which you paid interest during the year. Next, go through your credit card statements from last year to find out how much your annual fee was. Record these figures in the spaces provided. Finally, carefully review each of your statements from last year so as to identify any miscellaneous charges that may have been imposed (cash advance or convenience check fees, late-payment fees, over-the-limit charges, etc.). Fill in the amounts in the column provided. Now total these figures—both across and down. The totals in the far right-hand column represent how much a particular piece of plastic cost you last year. The totals at the bottom show you how much you paid in total interest charges, annual fees, or miscellaneous charges. Finally, add the cumulative figures at the bottom of each category together to derive your grand total. This figure reflects the total cost for all of your credit cards last year.

Most people are surprised to learn how much their credit cards cost them in just one year. The grand total you just calculated is only for one year's worth of plastic; imagine the cost over a three-to-five-year period! For many, this money could probably have been spent in many other, more worthwhile ways.

Credit Card	Interest Charges	Annual Fee	Misc. Charges	Totals
_____	$_____	+ $_____	+ $_____	= $_____
_____	$_____	+ $_____	+ $_____	= $_____
_____	$_____	+ $_____	+ $_____	= $_____
_____	$_____	+ $_____	+ $_____	= $_____
_____	$_____	+ $_____	+ $_____	= $_____
_____	$_____	+ $_____	+ $_____	= $_____

GRAND TOTAL = $_____

❑ Interest Rates

Fixed- vs. Variable-Rate Cards. Two types of interest rates are widely available on most credit cards today: fixed and variable. The interest charged on a fixed-rate card remains relatively constant. However, the rates on these cards are not totally "fixed." Unlike the truly fixed rates available on mortgages and car loans (which are essentially etched in stone), a fixed card's rate may be changed from time to time by the issuing institution. And, in many instances, a new, higher rate may be applied to your existing card balances. Since-most fixed rate cards are relatively static (the rate may be applicable over a several-year period), you normally do not have to worry about the rate changing often. Just understand that it might rise at some point in the future.

Because it is indexed to some other rate (for example, the six-month Treasury bill rate or the prime rate), a variable-rate card is designed to fluctuate with changing economic conditions. A variable-rate card will usually be set at so many percentage points above a base rate (such as prime plus 7 percent). This means that a low-variable-interest-rate card today might go higher or lower as the rate is adjusted (normally quarterly). However, since cardholders are free to cancel their cards at any time, variable-rate cards do not subject holders to significant risk. Just try to keep your card indebtedness well within your ability to repay should your rate go up considerably.

If your credit card issuer offers several different types of cards, you may be able to choose between fixed and variable rates and be allowed to select the card most suited to your needs and spending patterns. For example, you might choose a low-variable-interest-rate card with an annual fee if you know you will not pay your balances in full each month. Conversely, the same credit card issuer may also offer a no-annual-fee card with a higher interest rate that may be appropriate if you do not carry a balance on your card. As you shop around, you will undoubtedly find some institutions offering variable-rate cards and others offering fixed-rate cards.

The Importance of Interest Rates. Credit card interest rates may or may not be important to you depending upon your card usage and spending patterns. If you do not pay your credit card balance in full every month, the interest rate is perhaps the most important pricing component for you. If so, you need to find a card with a low interest rate. Similarly, if you use your credit card as a substitute for a personal loan (that is, if you carry a sizable balance due on your card most of the time), the interest rate assumes increased significance.

Bank card interest rates have remained high even though most other interest rates (such as mortgages and auto loans) have been consistently declining. In 1992, the average bank card interest rate declined slightly to about 18 percent, while

most lending rates were near twenty-year lows. For example, the average interest rate on a thirty-year fixed mortgage fell to a little over 7 percent. Personal, unsecured loans
could be obtained during this same period for about 16 percent, rates considerably lower than those charged on most
credit cards.

If you are carrying any level of card debt at high interest
rates, you should reevaluate your purchase decisions and
take action as soon as possible to reduce these expenses. Indeed, you could easily reap a high rate of return on an investment simply by paying off the outstanding balances on
many of your credit cards. Or you could switch to a card
with a lower interest rate. Both of these actions can save
you a bundle.

You probably need to gain a better understanding of
your existing situation before you can respond accordingly.
Do you even know the rates of interest you are currently
paying on your credit cards? To get a better handle on interest charges, enter your credit card information onto the
following table. For each creditor, write down the interest
rate(s) being charged. Since many creditors assess different
interest rates on purchases and cash advances, fill in the appropriate figures (purchases to the left of the slashes, advances
to the right). Then list the outstanding balance on each card.

Creditor	Interest Rates	Outstanding Balance	Repayment Priority
_____	____%/____%	$____/$____	___/___
_____	____%/____%	$____/$____	___/___
_____	____%/____%	$____/$____	___/___
_____	____%/____%	$____/$____	___/___
_____	____%/____%	$____/$____	___/___
_____	____%/____%	$____/$____	___/___

Start with cards having the highest interest rate. Since these are the obligations that ultimately will cost you the most, they should be designated as priority payments. The sooner you are able to pay them off, the less they will cost you. You can also make supplemental payments to your creditor and have these payments applied directly to the portion of your balance that carries the higher interest rate. For example, if you owe $1,000 on a cash advance at 19.8 percent and owe $2,000 on purchases at 15.9 percent on the same credit card, send in extra payments and earmark them to retire the higher rate cash advance balance first. You should check with your creditor concerning where to send these payments (some have special payments sections for this purpose). Specifically state in both your cover note and the "memo" section on your check that the money is to be applied toward the outstanding cash advance balance.

Develop a plan for lowering your credit card interest payments. This might include a combination of approaches. For example, if you have several credit cards with high interest rates, you might consider taking out a loan at a lower rate to repay these obligations. Or you might transfer your balances to another credit card offering a lower interest rate. If you are earning a low rate of interest on your savings, you might consider dipping into your savings to pay off your higher rate/higher cost credit cards (provided, however, you are not charged a penalty for early withdrawal). You could also develop a repayment strategy over a definite period of time. Under such a plan, you would make the minimum payments due on your lower interest rate obligations and supplemental payments on your higher interest rate obligations in an effort to repay those costing you the most money as quickly as possible. However you do it, you must take every action possible to reduce high-interest credit card debt.

❑ Annual Fees

Roughly a third of us are "convenience users" who pay our credit card bills in full each and every month. If you are among this group, the interest rate may not be very important to you. Instead, you may be more concerned about the availability of a long grace period and the amount of the annual fee.

Annual fees vary widely—ranging from zero to about $35 for regular cards, $50 or more for premium cards. Their applicability also varies. For example, some companies will waive the annual fee for the first year you hold the card; thereafter, an annual fee will be assessed. Consumers have been very successful in getting credit card companies to reduce or waive annual fees. In the face of powerful competitors like AT&T's Universal Card (which has granted a lifetime annual fee waiver for some of its customers), other issuers have been forced to take similar action. So the next time the annual fee charge shows up on your billing statement, call your credit card issuer. If you can get a similar card from someone else that does not have an annual fee, let your creditor know. To keep you as a customer, many are more than willing to meet or beat competitors' offers. But most are willing to grant a waiver for one year only; few will give you a lifetime waiver. So you may simply have to repeat the process each year when you get billed for the annual fee.

❑ Grace Periods

Many credit cards offer a grace period of varying lengths (often 25 to 30 days), during which you can pay off all new purchases without incurring finance charges. Be sure to get a card with a grace period if you normally pay your bill in full each month. Be aware, however, that you only benefit from a grace period if you start the billing cycle with a zero balance <u>and</u> you pay your entire bill each month by the due date. On most cards, all new purchases begin accruing finance charges immediately if you do not pay in full. If your card has a grace period, creditors must bill you at least fourteen days before your payment is due. This should allow you to make your payments by the due date so you can avoid interest charges.

Some credit card issuers have reduced or eliminated the grace period available on their cards. On cards without a grace period, finance charges will be assessed either from the date you make a purchase or from the date a transaction is posted to your account. If having the ability to "float" credit card charges interest-free through full payment each month is important to you, by all means find a card with a grace period. In addition, be aware that grace periods are usually available only on purchases you make with your credit card. On most cards, if you use a convenience check or get a cash advance, you are not entitled to any grace period and interest charges normally start accruing immediately.

❏ Balance Calculation Methods

The vast majority of credit card issuers use the "average daily balance (including new purchase)" balance calculation method. Under this approach, for each day of the billing cycle, the credit card issuer subtracts any payments and adds any new purchases made. The interest charged is based on the average of these daily loan balances. It is in your best interest to send credit card payments as early in the month as possible. This is because the earlier a payment is posted to your account, the lower the next month's average daily balance will be.

Very few credit card issuers use the "average daily balance (excluding new purchases)" method. This is similar to the calculation method above except that new purchases are not included when calculating the daily balance. In effect, issuers using this method extend an initial "grace period" even to customers who revolve their balances (do not pay their card balance in full each month and carry over balances from month to month).

Credit card issuers must identify their balance calculation method in the disclosure boxes on the card applications. So check the balance calculation method before applying. An additional item to watch out for is the daily compounding of interest. While this practice may be desirable on savings accounts, it is not desirable on credit cards.

A few credit card issuers, including Discover, Union Bank, Colonial National Bank, and some of Household Bank's accounts, use a "two-cycle average daily balance" calculation method. If you suspect you will occasionally revolve, these issuers should be avoided. Card issuers using this method will retroactively take away a grace period that they had previously extended and retroactively charge you interest for balances on the previous month's statement plus the regular finance charges for the current statement.

To illustrate, imagine that you charge a $1,000 purchase on your credit card, pay $800 upon receipt of the bill, and plan to pay the remainder the following month. In this example, the total finance charges would be almost four times higher for an issuer that uses two-cycle billing over an issuer who uses the standard average daily balance method. Once the total balance is paid off, the whole cycle starts all over again.

"One Cycle" Method

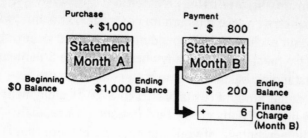

"Two Cycle" Method

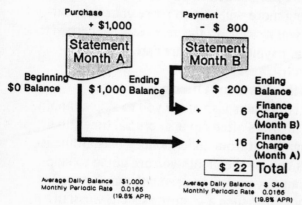

Figure 2 (One and Two Cycle Methods)

❑ Minimum Payment Requirements

Card issuers impose a minimum payment that is due on a certain date each month. Depending on the card issuer, the minimum payment will range anywhere from 2 to 5 percent of the outstanding balance. Some issuers also require a minimum dollar amount (usually $15 to $20) as a payment floor each month. Many credit card issuers have recently lowered the percentage of your outstanding balance that is required as a minimum payment. This means that on the same balance your required minimum payment each month may be smaller now than it was a couple of years ago. Your creditor makes more money because lower minimum payments extend the life of the loan for many months, during which time interest charges accumulate.

Given these widespread minimum payment practices, make every effort to pay off your credit card balances each month. If you cannot afford the full payment, pay as much as you can. You are not obliged to pay only the minimum amount due. Paying more will help to retire your debt earlier and will save you money. At the very least, be certain to make the minimum payment by the due date.

❑ "Skip a Month" Payment Offerings

Many credit card issuers also allow you to skip a month in payments. These offers often come at crucial times, like when you are digging out from under holiday bills. Some issuers even let you choose the month you are going to skip. While skipping your payment for one month may be useful on occasion, do not view such a gesture as a big windfall. Even though you may be able to skip a payment, interest charges will still be assessed throughout the period. Thus, skipping a month costs you money.

❏ Over-the-Limit Fees

Many institutions impose special charges that range from $5 to $20 for exceeding the credit limit. These charges are often imposed in spite of the fact that your credit card issuer may have authorized charges that place you over your limit. If you are over the limit and do not pay your balance in full, interest charges as well as over the limit fees will be assessed for each month in which this occurs. Since these costs are incurred for each billing period in which you are over the limit, they can take a tremendous cumulative toll. What's more, persistent over the limit problems can also result in the cancellation of your card. Being over the limit can also create some embarrassing moments with merchants if you attempt to use your card and it is declined.

If you are charged an over-the-limit fee, try to bring your indebtedness below your approved credit limit as soon as possible. You will need to somehow cough up the amount by which you exceed your limit plus the amount of the over-the-limit fee to get your account back in order. Should you have difficulty accomplishing this, determine the balance beyond which this fee is assessed. Some creditors assess an over-the-limit fee even if you go a penny beyond the credit limit; others charge if your balance exceeds your credit limit by 15 percent. Once this point has been determined, make every effort to bring your balance below it, and then strive to bring your indebtedness down below your approved credit limit. If you are unable to do both of these, contact the creditor to request that your credit limit be increased to the level of your current balances. This action will avoid further over-the-limit fees. If this is done, assure the creditor that account balances will remain below the revised credit limit.

❏ Late-Payment Fees

Many creditors assess late fees if payments are not received by a certain date each month. This date, which varies among creditors, is normally a number of days beyond the payment due date. For example, while some creditors may assess late-payment charges on the payment due date, most give a five-to-ten-day grace period beyond the payment due date for payments to be received and credited to an account. Late fees vary from creditor to creditor. Some charge a flat fee (usually $10 to $20 for each month in which you are late); others charge a percentage (usually around 2 percent) of the minimum payment due. Late fees are in addition to interest charges. Some creditors charge interest on the late fee amount; others do not.

If you are being assessed late-payment charges, try to submit payments before the due date. If you are cutting it close, contact the creditor to determine the monthly date when payments must be received in order to avoid these charges. Once your creditor's policy is determined, make every effort to ensure that your payments are credited by this date. If you cannot make a payment until the date on which the fee will be assessed, you might even consider hand-delivering the payment or sending it by messenger or overnight delivery. While this might wind up costing as much as the late fee, it might save you from having a late payment show up on your credit report—a liability that can follow you for years and impede future credit and loan applications.

If you feel a late-payment fee has been inappropriately assessed, call your credit card company and request that it be removed from your account. As a public relations gesture, many issuers are willing to give you the benefit of the doubt and grant you a one time waiver of the charge.

❑ Charges for Cash Advances and Convenience Checks

Almost all credit card issuers charge interest on cash advances and convenience checks. Some charge interest at the same rate as purchases; many assess higher interest rates for them. If your account has a grace period for purchases, the chances are pretty good that it does not apply to any cash advances you obtain or convenience checks you use. Interest charges on these items normally begin from the date of the advance or when the convenience check is posted.

Many institutions also assess a transaction fee each time you utilize cash advance and convenience check services. This fee will either be a fixed amount (from a minimum of $2 to a maximum of $20) or a percentage of the amount borrowed (2 to 2.5 percent of the total cash advance). On large cash advances or convenience checks, the cost can be substantial. If you make several of these types of transactions, the cumulative impact of these charges can be devastating. If these transactions are not paid in full in the next billing period, they may trigger interest charges on subsequent purchases.

You can see that convenience checks may not be so convenient after transaction charges are included. Therefore, do not use these checks (which in many cases require a $100 minimum) for just anything. If you are thinking about using them to transfer balances from higher rate cards to a lower rate card, contact your creditor and ask that the transaction charges for these checks be waived. Some issuers will do this on a per-request basis; others have blanket policies that waive these charges for just such consolidations.

❑ Transaction Charges

Some credit cards assess other types of charges, including monthly fees (whether you use the card or not), transaction fees (which are charged each time the card is used), and lost card replacement fees (typically $5; assessed when a card has been lost or stolen more than once or twice). Since most credit card issuers do not assess such fees, it should not be difficult to avoid those that do.

Shopping for Credit Cards

Armed with the valuable information you have now learned, shop around for the best credit card deals you can find. But first, take a good hard look at your credit needs and spending practices. For example, if you travel extensively, make certain to get a card that accommodates your on-the-road needs. Similarly, finding a card with extended warranty coverage on goods purchased may be important to you. If you need cash, a card with check-cashing privileges and access to ATM networks may be crucial. Select cards that are accepted at your favorite stores and restaurants. Find versatile cards that can be used in a multitude of places for a variety of purposes.

As you begin evaluating different products, you will probably quickly discover there are trade-offs to be made. You may find a card with no or a low annual fee, but it may come with strings attached, like no grace period or a high interest rate. Your best bet will probably be a "balanced" card, one with no gimmicks and moderately priced individual components.

You need not restrict yourself to local financial institutions. While a large number of financial services issuers still cater to local credit card customers, many financial institutions now market their products nationally and offer credit card products with very attractive terms. Bill payments and other consumer interaction with the credit card issuer are easily accomplished through the mail or over toll-free telephone numbers. You will likely get the same or better service from these national issuers as you would from a local establishment. What's more, even if you get your credit card from a local issuer, there is no assurance that the bank will not move its credit card operations to a distant state at some point in the future. Since most credit cards these days are exported to you from another state anyway, shop nationally and benefit from some of the best credit card deals in the country.

While shopping around for credit cards is an important ongoing activity, it is particularly timely if your current credit card issuer is increasing its interest rate, imposing a higher annual fee, eliminating or reducing the length of the grace period, or otherwise increasing your costs. In such instances, you are not obligated to keep existing credit cards. So if you think your credit card issuer's charges are too high, see if they will lower your interest rate or waive your annual fee. Many will respond favorably. If your credit card issuer refuses, perhaps you can do better somewhere else. If you qualify for lower cost credit cards, by all means cancel your current cards and start saving yourself some money. Let your credit card company know you are leaving because you have found a more attractive deal. If they know they are about to lose you, your existing credit card company may be willing to meet or beat the new offer or waive certain costs just to keep you as a customer. So it pays to be aggressive with your credit card company.

You also need to look behind the hype and gimmicks of some of the new, seemingly attractive credit card products to see if you really benefit from them. These offerings sometimes turn out to be far less advantageous than they originally appear. For example, a lower interest rate may only be

available to an issuer's best customers. Or the highly touted
interest rate may be a promotional rate available for a limited time only. Given such circumstances, you must do your
own research. Look behind the promotions to see if you really benefit from existing and new offerings.

Best Low-Interest/No-Fee Credit Cards Available

Four times a year, Bankcard Holders of America
(BHA), a nonprofit consumer advocacy group, compiles a
listing of the best low-interest/no-fee credit cards available
in the country. The information in this list is obtained from
an ongoing national survey of financial institutions across
the country. Reviewing this listing is probably one of the
best ways to start your credit card shopping. Here are some
of the best national card issuers on BHA's list for January
1993. *All but one of these are toll-free.*

Card	Interest Rate	Annual Fee	Grace Period	Phone Number
Abbott Bank (Neb.)	16.30%	—	25	800-999-6977
AFBA Industrial Bank (Va.)	12.50%	—	25	800-776-2322
Amalg. Bank of Chicago (Ill.)	12.00%	—	25	800-365-6464
Amer. Express Optima (Del.)	14.25%	$15	25	800-635-5955
Ark. Fed. Credit Card Svc.	8.00%	$35	None	800-477-3348
AT&T Universal (Fla.)	15.90%	$20	25	800-662-7759
Bank of New York (Del.)	11.90%	—	None	800-942-1977
Bank One, Columbus (Wis.)	13.90%	$25	25	800-388-0225
Chas. G. Givens Org. (Ark.)	7.75%	$37.50	25	800-284-4082
CHOICE (Md.)	13.40%	$20	25	800-733-2222
Consumer Ntl. Bankcard (Va.)	9.90%	—	25	800-862-1616
Discover (Ill.)	14.90%	—	25	800-347-2683

Card	Interest Rate	Annual Fee	Grace Period	Phone Number
Fidelity National Bank (Ga.)	17.90%	—	25	800-753-2900
First Consumer Bankcrd. (Va.)	6.90%	$29	25	800-952-3388
First National Bank (Ill.)	15.96%	$15	25	800-754-3202
First Natl. of Omaha (Neb.)	14.90%	$20	25	800-688-7070
First of America Bank (Mich.)	18.00%	—	25	800-423 3883
Ford/Assoc. Nat'l Bank (Del.)	18.40%	—	25	800-638-3673
Harris Bank (Ill.)	15.90%	—	25	800-445-4631
Household Bank (Calif.)	17.40%	—	25	800-477-6000
Natl. Bank of Savannah (N.Y.)	14.88%	$15	25	315-365-2896
Oak Brook Bank (Ill.)	10.40%	$20	25	800-666-1011
People's Bank (Conn.)	11.50%	$25	25	800-423-3273
Union Planter Bank (Tenn.)	14.75%	—	None	800-628-8946
USAA Fed. Savings (Okla.)	12.50%	—	25	800-922-9092
Wachovia Bank Card (Del.)	8.90%	$39	25	800-842-3262

BHA's full listing also includes the best credit cards available regionally. Since credit card prices tend to change fairly often, for the latest and most complete information contact Bankcard Holders of America, 1-800-553-8025. Upon request, BHA will send you the most up-to-date listing of financial institutions offering the best low-interest-rate or no-annual-fee credit cards. If you are interested in a secured card, BHA has a list of the best secured card deals available as well. A $4 fee is charged for each list. This modest cost pales in comparison to the money you will save by checking out the credit card deals identified by BHA. The organization, which offers a variety of other publications (including a $5 listing of the best gold cards), provides its publications and services free to its membership. For further information, contact:

Bankcard Holders of America
560 Herndon Pky, Suite 120
Herndon, VA 22070
(703) 481-1110

A couple of other credit cards of which you need to be aware are those offered by two major national membership organizations:

Card	Interest Rate	Annual Fee	Grace Period	Phone Number
AARP*	15.60%	$10	25	1-800-283-1211
AFL-CIO**	11.00%	- -	None	Contact local union

* Through Bank One, Columbus, Ohio
** Union Privilege, through Bank of New York, Del.

To qualify for either of these cards, you must be a member of these organizations. You might also check with other organizations to which you belong (for example, credit unions, professional organizations) to see if credit cards are offered. These offerings, which can often be quite favorable, are not available to the general public. As a result, they are not listed here.

Protecting Yourself on Current Obligations

☐ Keeping Credit Card Usage Within Reason

No one is suggesting that credit and credit cards should be avoided altogether. Everyone needs to gain access to credit in his or her life. Moreover, your creditworthiness—your ability to manage and control credit— is an important part of your identity. While having credit cards is important, you must not go overboard. There is no good reason for you to have a fistful of plastic at your disposal. You need only to gain access to sufficient credit to meet your needs and to respond to life's circumstances. With fewer cards, you will make fewer impulse purchases, have fewer bills to pay, be assessed fewer service charges and fees, be assessed less in interest charges, and suffer less inconvenience if your cards are lost or stolen.

If you do not keep your access to credit and your outstanding indebtedness within reason, potential creditors may refuse to give you additional credit. This could pose significant problems and result in the rejection of that all-important car loan or mortgage.

☐ Staying Current on Obligations

The best way to protect yourself on current obligations is to make timely payments according to the terms of your credit agreements. Follow your creditors' instructions concerning how, when, and where to make bill payments. Make sure your payments are mailed or delivered to the address specified by your creditor. If you pay by check, write your account number on the check. If there is no payment stub or detachable portion of a bill to return with your payment, include a note to your creditor indicating the date, amount of the payment attached, your account number, and your name and address. When your statement arrives, check promptly to make sure your payments have been properly credited to your account.

☐ Resolving Billing Disputes

If you find incorrect or duplicate entries on your credit card bill or do not receive proper credit for payments or returned items, you must quickly assert your rights with your creditor to have the matter resolved. There is no reason for you to have to pay or be penalized for someone else's billing mistake.

Carefully review your monthly billing statements from creditors. Billing errors occur. People make mistakes; so do computers. Compare your copies of receipts and check stubs with the charges and credits reflected on your statements promptly after they are received. If you notice an error, take the steps indicated below.

While a telephone call to your creditor might be helpful, such a call will not preserve your legal rights under the federal Fair Credit Billing Act. To do this, you must write your creditor within sixty days of the postmark date of a billing statement containing an error. Do not simply send your letter of dispute along with your payment. Rather, mail your letter separately to the address indicated on your statement for billing disputes. In your letter, make sure to:

- Include your name, address, and account number
- Indicate your belief that your statement contains a billing error
- Identify the amount of the billing error
- State your reasons for believing a billing error exists.

On receipt of your letter identifying a billing error, your creditor must do the following:

- Acknowledge receipt of your letter within thirty days; or
- Conduct a reasonable investigation within two billing cycles (but no longer than ninety days) and either make appropriate corrections to your account or send you an explanation of why a billing error does not exist or why you still owe a portion of the disputed amount.

During these periods, you do not have to pay the amount in dispute, including finance charges and minimum payments relating to the disputed matter. You must, however, make other payments required under your credit agreement on undisputed charges. While the dispute is being resolved, your creditor may not initiate collection activities against you, restrict or close your account, or make an adverse report to a credit-reporting agency because of your failure to pay the disputed amount. The disputed amount may be counted toward your credit limit and a creditor is free to pursue collection activities on undisputed amounts.

☐ Protection Against Defective Merchandise

If you purchase merchandise that turns out to be defective or of inferior quality, return the merchandise to the place where you bought it and give the seller the opportunity either to replace the item or refund your money. You must make a good-faith effort to obtain satisfactory resolution of the disagreement or problem from the seller.

What if the merchant refuses? For cash or check payments, you might pursue your rights under your state's laws. But if you made the purchase with a credit card, you may be entitled to additional rights under the Fair Credit Billing Act. In such cases, your rights will still be determined by the laws of the state in which you live. The Fair Credit Billing Act, however, may extend these state provisions.

You may be allowed to enforce the same legal actions against your credit card issuer that you have under state law against the seller of the merchandise. For example, if your state law allows you to withhold payment to a seller of defective merchandise, you might be able to withhold payment to your credit card issuer. Thus, you should first check with a local attorney to determine what defenses-to-payment protections are afforded under your state's laws. You will

then be able to assert these state-allowed defenses against
both the seller and the credit card issuer, provided: (1) you
purchased the item in your home state or within one hundred miles of your current billing address and (2) the
amount of the purchase is greater than $50.

☐ Protecting Yourself Against Credit and Charge Card Theft and Fraud

If your credit or charge cards are lost or stolen, immediately notify your credit card issuers. Most have toll-free
numbers and twenty-four-hour service available for this purpose. You should follow up with a letter advising your
creditor in writing of the loss or theft. In this correspondence, indicate your name and card number, the precise time
and date you discovered your card missing, and the time and
date you reported the lost or stolen card to your creditor.

Under the federal Truth-in-Lending Act, you cannot be
held responsible for any charges made to your cards after
you have reported them lost or stolen. Even though your
maximum liability can never exceed $50 per card, the earlier
you act, the greater the likelihood you will be able to limit
your out-of-pocket expenses and the unauthorized user's
access to your credit. If several credit cards are lost or stolen, your maximum liability can quickly mount up. After reporting a credit or charge card loss or theft, review subsequent billing statements carefully and contest any unauthorized charges.

To protect yourself against credit card theft and fraud
problems, take these precautions:

- ○ Sign new credit cards as soon as they arrive.
- ○ Keep all your credit card account numbers, expiration dates, and card issuer phone numbers and addresses in a secure place.

○ Notify card companies immediately if cards are lost or stolen. Consider buying a subscription to one of the many card registration services that will cancel your credit cards if they are lost or stolen.

○ Keep your credit cards in a safe place when carrying them with you.

○ Keep your credit cards in a safe place when not in use. Since you can usually anticipate your spending needs, do not routinely carry all of your credit cards. Rather, if you know you may go to a particular store and make a purchase, take your store charge card with you. Then immediately remove it from your wallet or pocketbook when you return.

○ Watch your card when you give it to a salesperson. Make sure it is used only for your transaction; be certain the card you receive back is yours; put your card in a safe place immediately on its return (for example, do not leave it on the counter while the clerk is packaging your purchase). Keep an eye on your wallet or pocketbook while the clerk is processing your transaction.

○ Save all records of transactions. Carefully scrutinize the charge slip. Is your account number reflected? Are all the amounts listed (usually there are hand written as well as printed totals) correct? Draw a line through any blank spaces where additional amounts might be inserted. Avoid signing a blank, imprinted credit card sales slip.

○ If carbons are used with your transaction, make sure to tear them up and take them with you. If the clerk makes a mistake and has to redo the charge slip, make certain the first paperwork is destroyed in your presence. Similarly, if an electronic approval was obtained, be sure it is canceled before the second authorization goes through.

○ Be careful with what happens to your copies of credit card receipts once you get them home. Never simply toss them in the trash. Tear them up before discarding them. Do not leave credit cards or receipts lying around your home or workplace. Keep them in a safe place, out of view.

○ Never give your credit card number or its expiration date to anyone over the a phone unless you are sure of the company's legitimacy or you initiate the call. Should you be enticed by the offering of someone who calls you, ask the caller to put the offering in writing and to provide you with either an address or phone number where you can contact them. If you are not familiar with a particular company, call your local consumer protection office, Better Business Bureau, or your state attorney general's office before ordering.

○ Be discreet if you initiate a call and give your credit card number to someone over the phone. Do not allow anyone within earshot to overhear your number.

○ Open billing statements promptly and reconcile your card accounts each month.

○ Make sure to notify your credit card companies in advance of a change of address.

○ Never lend your credit or charge cards or give your account numbers to anyone else.

○ Never write your account number on a postcard, the outside of a letter, your office Rolodex, or any other such place. When mailing your payments, make certain your account number is not visible through the envelope.

R E C O M M E N D A T I O N S

Credit cards play a significant role in our lives. They give us convenience and flexibility to respond to a variety of circumstances. There are different types of credit cards with which you need to be familiar—bank, charge, retail, and secured cards. The major factors influencing credit card costs are interest rate, annual fee, grace period, balance calculation method, minimum payment amount, late-payment and over-the-limit fees. Many cards also offer product enhancements which should be factored into your credit card selection decision.

Credit card costs can take a considerable bite out of your budget. It is important, therefore, to understand these costs and to reduce them wherever possible. Shop around for a credit card that meets your needs and spending patterns. One of the best ways to do this is to get the most recent copy of Bankcard Holders of America's no- and low-fee credit cards listing.

Should you have problems with a credit card, you need to learn how to resolve billing disputes, how to contest payments for defective merchandise, and how to protect yourself against credit and charge card theft and fraud.

NOTES

10

Installment, Home Equity, and Other Loans

Marty is considering trading in his two-year old car for a new one. Even though his car is in pretty good condition, he still has two years to go on a loan at a rate in excess of 10 percent. With many promotional rates on car loans now much lower, Marty can probably find a better interest rate if he buys a new car. He might also consider refinancing his current loan at a lower rate.

Kelly is interested in taking out a loan to finance a variety of needs in her life: a long-needed vacation, home and automobile repairs, braces for her teenage son, and some new furniture. Since she has amassed considerable equity in her home through twelve years of mortgage payments, Kelly should seriously consider applying for a home equity loan. Its interest rate should be much lower than what she can find on other loans. What's more, she should be able to deduct her interest payments on her taxes.

In addition to credit cards, a vast array of other credit products exist. Among these are lines of credit and install-ment, automobile, and home equity loans. Within these cat-egories you will find different pricing characteristics. These include secured, unsecured, closed-end, open-end, fixed-rate, and variable-rate loans. It is important to understand these different types of loans.

Common Loan Pricing Characteristics

❏ Secured vs. Unsecured Loans

Secured loans require collateral. On a new-car loan, for example, the vehicle serves as collateral for the financial in-stitution granting the loan. The lender holds the title, retains a security interest, and is free to repossess the vehicle in case of default. Other examples of secured loans are boat loans, home furniture or appliance loans, home equity loans, and mortgages.

An unsecured loan does not require collateral. For ex-ample, you may take out a personal, unsecured loan at a lo-cal financial institution to take a vacation. While your credi-tor can come after you personally should a default occur, it does not acquire a vested or special interest in the things you purchase with the loan proceeds.

Given the fact that creditors are better protected under a secured loan, most are more likely to lend money for this kind of loan. Conversely, since an unsecured loan is not attached to collateral, lenders are often less willing to extend credit. Rates on secured loans are also normally lower than rates on unsecured loans. For example, in November 1992, the average interest rate banks were charging on a forty-eight-month new-car loan was 8.6 percent, while the average rate on a twenty-four-month unsecured, personal loan stood at 13.55 percent. That is a spread of almost five percentage points between the secured and the unsecured loan rates.

The quality of the security or collateral pledged also influences a lender's interest rate. Generally, the greater the likelihood that the security can be easily used by the lender (in the event of default), the lower the loan rate. The highest quality collateral objects are assets controlled by the lending institution, such as the cash value of a whole-life insurance policy or a CD. In case of default, the lender can easily liquidate these assets to recover the loan principal and related expenses. The lowest quality collateral objects are assets that can easily depreciate in value, such as home furniture, appliances, and automobiles. Newer objects tend to retain their resale value much better than older, used objects. Since items under your control are obviously outside of a lender's direct control, they can be destroyed or seriously damaged through misuse or abuse. In addition, normal wear and tear will often take a considerable bite out of an object's value. Obviously, the quality of this type of collateral is lower than that of assets held directly by the lender.

While secured loans normally yield the lowest rates and may be easier to obtain, personal, unsecured loans are still quite common. In fact, many lenders aggressively advertise for bill or credit card consolidation loans. As a result, there are quite a few good deals available from financial institutions on personal, unsecured loans. The rates on these loans are normally several percentage points below the interest rates on many credit cards. On a personal, unsecured loan, you may also have to meet higher qualification standards than would normally be the case for a secured loan. Thus, your credit history may assume increased significance. In addition, most unsecured loans are for relatively short periods of time (usually from one to three years). While some longer term loans are available, be cautious of them, since they tend to be from finance companies at exorbitant rates of interest.

❑ Closed-End vs. Open-End Loans

Closed-end loan plans are for a set period of time for a fixed dollar amount. For example, a two-year $5,000 personal, unsecured loan is a closed-end loan, since neither the length of the loan nor its amount will change. The balance will be repaid in equal monthly installments over a twenty-four-month period. Open-end loans, on the other hand, allow you to revolve. For example, you may have $1,000 in overdraft protection on a line of credit attached to your checking account. Since you can access and repay your loan without having to apply for a new loan, your line of credit represents an open-end loan.

❑ Fixed- vs. Variable-Rate Loans

In chapter 9, fixed- and variable-rate credit cards were discussed. Many of the same principles apply to loans as well. There is one significant difference, however, between fixed-rate cards and fixed-rate loans. Fixed-rate credit cards are not truly fixed, since they can be changed from time to time by the card issuer. Fixed-rate loans, on the other hand, normally cannot be altered by the lender once the loan agreement has been signed.

Both fixed- and variable-rate loans abound. If interest rates are low, you might opt for a fixed-rate loan that will lock you in to the best interest rate available on the loan date. If interest rates then go up or down, your interest rate will remain the same. You will be able to pay off your obligation at your contracted rate irrespective of changing economic conditions. With a variable-rate loan, the interest rate fluctuates with changes in the index used by the institution. At most institutions, the interest rate is based upon some external index, such as the three-month Treasury bill or the prime lending rate. Some institutions, however, tie the rate to the institution's own internal index or cost of funds. Thus, while other interest rates may be declining, the institution can increase its own index, thereby increasing your interest costs. For this reason, try to avoid variable-rate loans that are based upon an institution's internal index.

While you should feel free to pursue fixed- or variable-rate loans, steer clear of long-term variable-rate loans. Short-term variable-rate loans are acceptable because there is very little chance that rates will skyrocket in one, two, or three years. Since no one knows what will happen to interest rates in fifteen to thirty years, do not commit yourself to such a variable rate loan. If interest rates rise significantly, so will your loan payments. This might strain your available resources and wind up costing you a bundle. If you are forced to refinance, you will probably have to do so at a rate significantly higher than what you can currently obtain.

Types of Loans

❑ Lines of Credit
Roughly half of the financial institutions in this country

offer an unsecured revolving credit line that is linked to a
personal account. This is the most popular type of line of
credit, also known as overdraft protection. A limited number of institutions also offer a credit line not linked to an account but accessible through special checks or line activa-
tors.

A line of credit is an open-end credit plan that allows
you to make repeated transactions on the same account,
provided you stay within your established credit limit. Even
though such plans normally require periodic, automatic payments, you should be able to make payments toward your
outstanding balance at any time. Depending upon your financial institution, minimum monthly payments will be
based upon a percentage of your outstanding balance (usually 2.5 to 5 percent) or a fixed monthly amount (anywhere
from $20 to $50). Interest charges are assessed on your unpaid balance. The average rates charged on variable rate
lines of credit are between 9.5 and 15 percent; on fixed-rate
lines of credit, from 14 to 18 percent. In addition to interest,
some institutions assess an annual fee of $15 to $50 for line
of credit accounts. A limited number charge an application
fee (usually around $25).

Using overdraft protection on a bank account as an example, here is how a line of credit works. You are provided
a preapproved credit limit that you can utilize through transactions on your account. With this you can essentially write
yourself a loan by overdrawing your account. Instead of
having your checks bounce, you are covered up to your approved limit. During the months in which you have an outstanding balance, most financial institutions will automatically debit your monthly minimum payments from your
checking account and credit this amount toward your line of
credit balance. You can repeat this process whenever you

wish, just so long as you stay within your approved line of credit amount.

❏ Installment Loans

Unlike the open-end line of credit discussed above, an installment loan is a closed-end credit plan. This means that you get a loan for a predetermined loan amount. You are not able to pay down the indebtedness and reborrow as under the line of credit discussed above. Rather, you are required to pay the loan amount off under a repayment plan of a set amount per month for a fixed period. For example, suppose you take out a $1,000 installment loan at 16 percent interest for one year. During this year, you will be expected to make payments of $90.74 per month. The total cost of the loan including principal and interest: $1,088.88.

Installment loans can be used for financing a vacation, paying for home or auto repairs, purchasing home appliances and furniture, and buying a car. They can also be quite useful when paying off high-interest-rate credit cards or when used as a general bill consolidation loan. Through these two latter types of loans, bill payments may be simplified with a single monthly payment to one creditor. These payments, which are normally stretched out over a two-to-three-year period, may be lower than the bills you were paying individually each month. This could give you a little more flexibility in meeting monthly obligations and in responding to emergencies. If you are interested in an installment loan, check around with several financial institutions to see what they offer and select the one most appropriate for you. While some merchants and many finance companies offer installment loans, be cautious of the interest rates they often charge—often 20 percent and upward. Your best bet will probably be with financial institutions, which often offer installment loans on the most reasonable terms available.

Rates on personal, unsecured loans have been falling in recent years. The average interest rate charged by banks on a twenty-four-month loan fell from about 15.5 percent in late 1990 to around 13.5 percent two years later. In today's environment, you should be able to find some quite attractive installment loans with favorable rates. If a prospective loan's rate is 15 percent or higher, reconsider applying for this loan. With good deals to be had these days, there is really no reason to accept installment loan rates much higher than about 15 percent. This rule of thumb also applies to merchants who are willing to finance purchases you make from them at 18 to 21 percent interest. You would be far better off avoiding merchant financing and getting a personal, unsecured loan at a much lower interest rate at a financial institution or using a low-interest-rate credit card instead.

❏ **Automobile Loans**

The automobile loan is perhaps the best known secured installment loan. There is tremendous variation in the interest rates currently available on car loans. Some of the best deals around can be found through automobile dealer financing. The rates financial institutions charge on car loans tend to be higher. This is because car dealers, who are often quite anxious to sell cars, will sometimes offer very attractive financing terms (some as low as 2.9 percent). Many of these rock-bottom rates, however, are promotional and are only available on select models for a limited time period. Many of these super-discounted rates, which also carry a short repayment period (often two years), require a substantial down payment. What's more, in many instances you are required to have an exemplary credit record. If you can qualify for and afford the payments on one of these promotional rates, this may be a good car-financing option for you. Even if you do not qualify for one of these extra-special promotional rates, you may still be able to find a pretty good deal through automobile dealer financing.

Interest rates on automobile loans have dropped considerably in recent years. For example, the average interest rate charged by banks on a forty-eight-month new-car loan was almost 12 percent in late 1990; by late 1992, it had fallen to about 8.5 percent. That is a drop of three and a half percentage points in a two-year span! The length of loans available to finance cars has also increased of late, with loans of forty-eight to sixty months or longer now fairly common.

Many financial institutions are aggressively soliciting new-car loan business by offering attractive interest rates. For example, early in 1993, First American Bank in Washington, D.C., was advertising forty-eight-month new-car loans at a promotional rate of 7.25 percent, well below the industry average. What's more, in an effort to gain your car-financing business, many banks these days are offering loans that allow you to refinance your existing car loan. Under such plans, you may be able to refinance an existing 10 percent car loan at 7.5 to 8.5 percent. Thus, you may be able to save money on the ultimate cost of your car while reducing your monthly payments. If you have an existing car loan that you feel is too high, shop around to see if you qualify for automobile refinancing. Refinancing is only available through financial institutions; automobile dealers do not refinance cars.

If you obtain an automobile loan from a financial institution, you may also be able to shave off anywhere from one-quarter to a full percentage point on your interest rate by authorizing automatic bill payments or maintaining other account relationships with the lending institution. This can further decrease your car's ultimate cost and diminish your monthly car payments even more.

The following listing identifies some of the best new-car loan rates available from financial institutions across the country at the end of December 1992.

BEST AUTOMOBILE LOANS AVAILABLE IN THE LARGEST METROPOLITAN AREAS

Region	Institution	Rate/Term as of Dec. 92	Telephone
Atlanta	South Trust Bank	7.50% / 48 mos.	(404) 423-3435
Baltimore	Loyola Federal Savings	7.50% / 60 mos.	(410) 332-7000
Boston	U.S. Trust	8.49% / 48 mos.	(617) 849-9700
Chicago	Lakeshore National Bank	6.75% / 48 mos.	(312) 787-1900
Cleveland	Horizon Savings	8.50% / 60 mos.	(216) 765-1100
Dallas	North Dallas Bank & Trust	7.50% / 36 mos.	(214) 387-1300
Denver	Omnibank Southeast	6.90% / 36 mos.	(303) 773-1234
Detroit	First State Bank	8.00% / 60 mos.	(313) 775-5000
Houston	First Heights Bank	7.75% / 48 mos.	(713) 869-3411
Los Angeles	Community Bank	8.25% / 60 mos.	(818) 577-1700
Miami	San Bank/Miami	8.00% / 36 mos.	(305) 592-0800
Minneapolis	Metropolitan Federal Bank	8.50% / 60 mos.	(612) 339-7276
N. Y. City	Independence Savings	7.75% / 48 mos.	(718) 624-6620
North N.J.	National Community Bank	7.95% / 36 mos.	(201) 357-7000
Philadelphia	Frankford Trust	8.00% / 48 mos.	(215) 831-6400
Phoenix	Primerit Bank	7.75% / 48 mos.	(800) 537-8654
Pittsburgh	Community Savings Bank	7.50% / 60 mos.	(412) 664-8795
St. Louis	United Missouri Bank	7.90% / 48 mos.	(314) 522-6900
San Diego	Grossmont Bank	8.50% / 60 mos.	(619) 462-2800
San Francisco	Citibank	8.50% / 60 mos.	(415) 981-3180
Seattle	Key Bank of Washington	8.50% / 60 mos.	(206) 447-5758

Region	Institution	Rate/Term as of Dec. 92	Telephone
SW Conn.	Gateway Bank	8.50% / 48 mos.	(203) 853-2265
Tampa	First Gulf Bank	7.75% / 60 mos.	(813) 525-3441
Wash. DC	First Virginia Bank	7.50% / 60 mos.	(703) 241-4000

Source: Money Magazine, February 1993 (as reported by HSH Associates). Rate and terms apply only to new car loans of $10,000. Pricing components on other loans will vary.

❑ Home Equity Loans

Home equity loans can take the form of either secured installment loans or secured lines of credit. Under a home equity loan, your lending institution acquires a security interest in your home up to the amount of your loan. In the event of a default, you could lose your home. This is because your home serves as collateral for the loan. The principal danger with these loans is that credit limits are usually so high that families may increase their debt well beyond prudent levels. In doing so, they may substantially reduce their home equity, the principal savings for many households.

In recent years, home equity loans have become a very popular lending product. This is because after the 1986 federal tax reform law these loans have become one of the last remaining tax loopholes available to consumers. You are generally able to deduct interest expenses you pay on a home equity loan (although certain exceptions do exist). If interest deductibility is important to you, consult with a tax advisor before applying for a home equity loan.

Many financial institutions are now vigorously advertising for home equity loan business. Creative, new home equity loan products, with varying features, are frequently emerging. Variable-interest home equity loans abound; others come with fixed interest rates; some offer low monthly payments with balloon payments at the end of the loan.

With some home equity loans, you can even write checks or use a credit card that accesses the equity you have in your home. Preapproved lines of credit attached to your home's equity hold forth the promise of never having to apply for another loan.

Since products vary tremendously, you must carefully evaluate home equity loan offerings. Shop around to find the loan that best suits your individual needs. If your borrowing needs are relatively small, you might consider pursuing a personal, unsecured loan or using savings instead. Do not apply for a home equity loan if you are in any way irresponsible with money. The risks are simply too great to play around with the equity in your home.

Many of the current home equity products are variable-interest offerings which appear to carry very low interest rates. Many of these are simply promotional rates, available through a certain date or for a set period of time (normally ninety days). Thereafter, the actual rate will usually be indexed to an outside rate, like the prime lending rate, with a specified percentage added. Thus, you may only benefit from the promotional rate for a short period of time, with the bulk of your loan coming at a substantially higher interest rate. This actual rate, however, may still be lower than anything else you can obtain on the market. Since your indebtedness is linked to an outside index, you might be subjected to higher or lower interest rates in the future.

If you take out a variable-rate home equity loan, you should be wary of the uncertainties of changing economic conditions. Do not take out a long-term home equity loan just on the off chance that interest rates will remain low. Should you obtain an open-end home equity loan, do not use more of your approved line of credit than you can realistically repay in a couple of years. Or take out a short-term, closed-end loan of two to three years. Then, if interest rates skyrocket, you should be able to pay off your obligations fairly quickly. If you need to borrow more money, you will be able to base your decision on the economic conditions of the time rather than being locked into a high interest rate under a long-term loan.

Home equity loans carry the same sorts of expenses you would normally encounter when buying a house (closing costs, appraisal fees, title, points, attorney's fees). Other costs your lender may attach to the loan may include application fees, annual fees, transaction charges, prepayment penalties, and other service charges.

Many home equity loans require relatively high minimum loan amounts, normally $5,000 or more. Some loans also carry maximum or minimum withdrawal requirements. In addition, lenders place an outside limit on the percentage of equity in your home you can access. Most lenders will only allow you to borrow around 75 to 80 percent of your home's current market value, minus any encumbrances (like your first mortgage and any second mortgages). If you just purchased a new home, you may have very little equity built up. If you have your house almost paid for or are well into a long-term mortgage, you may have considerable equity at your disposal. Some lenders have higher income requirements for home equity loans than for unsecured loans. If your loan has a variable interest rate, you should check to see whether you are allowed to convert it to a fixed rate.

With interest rates in the range of 6 to 8 percent at many financial institutions, home equity loans are normally well below the interest rates charged on most other loan products. Compare these rates to the average rates charged on other popular loan products: credit cards, 18 percent 24-month personal, unsecured loan, 13.5 percent; forty-eight-

month new-car loan, 8.6 percent. It is obvious that home
equity loans are some of the most attractive loan products
available today. The following listing identifies some of the
best home equity loan rates available across the country.

BEST HOME EQUITY LINES OF CREDIT AVAILABLE IN THE LARGEST METROPOLITAN AREAS

Region	Institution	Rate as of Dec. 30, 1992	Telephone Number
Atlanta	Prime Bank	7.50%	(404) 370-8600
Baltimore	Chase Bank of Maryland	6.70%	(800) 242-7325
Boston	Boston Federal Savings	7.50%	(617) 273-0300
Chicago	First American Bank	7.00%	(708) 228-5505
Cleveland	Horizon Savings	7.50%	(216) 765-1100
Denver	Bank One	8.00%	(303) 292-4000
Detroit	Oakland Commercial Bank	8.00%	(313) 855-0550
Los Angeles	National Bank	7.50%	(310) 595-5281
Miami	Coral Gables Federal Savings	8.00%	(305) 447-4711
Minneapolis	First Banks	8.00%	(612) 244-3900
New York City	Republic National Bank	6.00%*	(800) 522-5214
N. New Jersey	Investors Savings Bank	7.00%	(201) 376-5100
Philadelphia	Beneficial Mutual Savings	7.50%	(215) 864-3535
Phoenix	Caliber Bank	7.50%	(602) 640-9400
Pittsburgh	West View Savings	6.60%	(412) 935-7170
St. Louis	First Bank	7.50%	(314) 567-3600
San Diego	First Interstate Bank	6.00%*	(800) 622-4430
San Francisco	Union Bank	7.00%	(415) 445-0225
Seattle	Pacific First Bank	8.00%	(206) 224-3530
SW Conn.	First Federal Bank	5.90%*	(203) 755-1422
Tampa	The Bank of Tampa	7.90%	(813) 872-1200
Wash. DC	Citizens Bank & Trust	6.50%*	(301) 206-6100
National	Prudential Bank & Trust	6.00%	(800) 426-4331

Source: Money Magazine, February 1993 (as reported by HSH Associates). All rates indicated are variable. ' Rate good for first year only.

RECOMMENDATIONS

You need to understand the differences in the various types of loans available today: secured, unsecured, closed-end, open-end, fixed-rate, variable-rate loans. Then find the loan best suited to your needs. The type of loan you select will depend upon the goods and services you wish to purchase.

If you use a line of credit, you need to be aware of the costs associated with its use and conform your activities to reduce loan costs. When considering an installment loan, try to benefit from some of the low-cost loans available and stay away from the much more costly installment loans you may encounter. There is a lot of price competition today on automobile loans. Shop around for your loan just as you do for the car. If you already have an existing high-rate car loan, consider refinancing at a lower rate. Home equity loans can be quite attractive because of their low rates and the deductibility of interest. However, proceed cautiously with a home equity loan. Never forget that a default can result in loss of the home. You also need to be aware of the significant costs associated with home equity loans.

NOTES

11

Electronic Banking

When Marion recently pulled into a gas station for a fill up, she realized that she had left her money and credit cards at home. Instead of returning home to retrieve these items, she simply used the ATM card in her wallet to pay for her gasoline. The amount of her purchase was automatically debited from her checking account balance.

Mike hates to sit down, write out checks, lick stamps, and mail in his monthly bill payments. As an alternative, he subscribes to a bill payment service that automatically makes his payments for him each month.

Edith is a Social Security recipient who used to take the bus down to her local bank to deposit her monthly Social Security check. Since enrolling in direct deposit, she no longer has to make this trip or stand in long bank

lines. Her money is now electronically credited to her
account without her having to lift a finger.

You may already have a vast array of electronic banking
services and features available at your fingertips. Automated
teller machines, debit/point-of-sale cards, direct deposits, direct withdrawals/automatic payments, telephone bill payment services, account information lines, home banking by
computer, and other devices are becoming part of a host of
electronic technologies that are now or will soon be available to millions of consumers. Many of these services are
provided through what is known in banking circles as electronic funds transfers (EFTs).

To maximize your position in this exciting new electronic banking environment, you need to learn how to avail
yourself of these enhanced capabilities. This should enable
you to streamline financial management duties, eliminate unnecessary time and effort spent on financial chores, shop for
more favorable rates on financial products, and enhance personal safety. These services will also allow you to conduct
banking activities virtually anytime, anywhere.

You should also learn more about the latest financial
management and bill payment software for personal computers that is available for general purchase. Telephone
companies, consumer electronics companies, software companies, and others also provide varying types of "information services" offerings that allow you to conduct banking
transactions over the telephone. Armed with the latest information and requisite tools, you will be able to put state-of-
the-art computer know-how to work for you.

You also need to understand your rights and how to enforce them should problems with any of these new services arise.

Electronic Banking Services

❑ Automated Teller Machines (ATMs)

If you are like most Americans, you may have come to
rely upon the thousands of self-service automated teller machines (ATMs) that dot the country. Some are positioned
outside or in the lobbies of financial institutions. Others can
be found in grocery and convenience stores, airports, work
locations, shopping malls, and other places where daily activities take us. These machines allow you to conduct many
of your banking activities twenty-four hours a day.

Not only are ATMs handy locally, but you can often
withdraw money from your financial institution even when
you are thousands of miles away. For example, you can
withdraw money on your bank account in New York from
ATMs in California (and vice versa). This is because your
local financial institution probably participates in shared
ATM networks (such as Cirrus, Plus, or MAC). These link
the ATM networks of various institutions so you can obtain
services at machines throughout the system. Many provide a
handy booklet that identifies locations where your ATM
card is accepted (this may include thousands of places
worldwide). Some networks even operate toll-free numbers
that access operators who will give you the location of the
nearest network machine. Or you can key in the zip code
where you are and a computer will locate the network machines nearest you.

Whether you use the ATM around the corner, across the
country, or in another part of the world, these machines offer convenience at your fingertips. You can often avoid having to go into a bank lobby, averting the hassles of waiting

in long lines to transact your business. With their increasing popularity, however, you often find fairly long lines at ATMs during peak periods at prime locations. These still usually pale in comparison to the lines found inside financial institutions.

ATMs allow you to accomplish a host of activities, which vary by institution. Permissible activities might include: obtaining account balances, withdrawing money (usually in $10 or $20 increments, with daily allowable limits ranging from $200 to $500), making deposits, reviewing past account activities, transferring money between accounts, paying bills, putting stop-payment orders on checks, getting statement printouts, and purchasing other financial products (like CDs). Some of the newest machines can even read and cash checks. Indeed, you are now able to perform on ATMs many services previously available only from tellers in the lobby.

Some of these machines are even multilingual. For example, Citibank's ATMs can be programmed to speak twenty-nine different languages (although only five are frequently used). Older generation machines with separate keypads for making selections are now being replaced by second-generation machines that provide a series of on-screen prompts from which to make selections. Instead of touching a keypad, you touch the appropriate spaces on the computer screen.

To access ATMs, you must first fill out an application with your financial institution, which then issues a debit ATM card. As a security precaution, a personal identification number (PIN) is normally issued as well. While some institutions will arbitrarily issue you a short four-to-six-digit PIN, others will let you choose your own number. With your card in hand and your security access code in mind, banking activities are only a couple of keystrokes away.

ATM prices vary. Some institutions allow you unlimited transactions for using machines at their branches. Others give you a set number of transactions at bank-owned machines but charge you for transactions in excess of the allowable number. Most will charge you an additional fee if you use a network machine that is not owned by your financial institution (anywhere from $.50 to $2). A limited number of financial institutions allow you a certain number of free network transactions per month but will assess per-transaction charges if you exceed the allowable number.

While ATM fees may appear to be fairly low, they can quickly mount up. Since most financial institutions do not group ATM charges so they are easily understood, these transaction charges are often buried in your bank statement. As a result, you have to scrutinize carefully your bank statement to find them. To gain a healthier appreciation for just how much ATM fees may be costing you, go through your most recent statements and total up your ATM charges. Remember, these charges are on top of your monthly account maintenance fee and other charges. To save yourself money, learn your bank's ATM pricing policy and conform your activities to reduce these costs.

Since ATM services differ from institution to institution, it is important to shop around. Pay particular attention to the following factors:

○ Does the financial institution's ATM and its network offer the specific services you desire? Can you transfer funds between your checking and savings accounts? Does the financial institution provide a wide range of services?

○ Are machines available in convenient locations? Are they easily accessible from your home and workplace?

Are they in neighborhoods that you frequent (near your favorite restaurants, near the homes or offices of friends and relatives)? Does the network service places to which you may travel?

O Are the ATMs easy to use? Are the instructions simple and clear? Can you read the screens? If you are physically impaired, are machines fully accessible? Does the ATM speak your language?

O Can the ATMs be used in privacy? It is very impor tant that no one can read your identification number as you punch it in. With your PIN and ATM card, a thief can easily steal funds from your accounts.

O Does the ATM take a photo of each use of the machine? This photo provides a record of people who make transactions and can be helpful if your card is lost, stolen, or used by someone without your permission.

O Are the machines located in well-lighted, glass-enclosed vestibules accessible only to those with ATM cards? Are there telephones nearby to reach customer service representatives? ATM location and placement are particularly important to those who need to use them at night or in high-crime areas. Some financial institutions even post armed guards at certain ATM locations.

O Does the financial institution assess transaction charges for using ATMs? What are ATM costs per transaction at your bank's ATMs and at network machines? What are the cost/convenience trade-offs of ATM usage?

❑ **Point-of-Sale Debit Cards**

Your ATM card is a debit card that allows you to access
your deposited funds through ATMs. With a debit card, the
amount of your transaction is automatically deducted from a
checking, savings, money market, or other deposit account
you maintain with the institution that issued the card. The financial institution is not lending you money; it simply allows
you to access funds in your account via a debit card. If you
do not have a sufficient balance to cover the transaction, it
may be declined. While transaction fees may or may not be
assessed (depending upon your institution's policy), you do not
pay interest charges because you are taking your own money.
Since this comes directly out of your bank account, you
need to reconcile your bank statement accordingly by sub-
tracting the amount of the transaction from your account ledger.

Historically, your ATM card could only be used to obtain cash and transact other business with a financial institution. This is still the case for many financial institutions
across the country. Even though some tremendous changes
are currently taking place (see below), you will still be able
to use your existing card at ATMs to get cash and transact
your banking business just as before. Not all financial institutions plan to expand their existing ATM card capabilities,
but many of your local institutions will probably start offering new debit card services at some point in the future;
some are already doing so. Therefore, if availing yourself of
these latest technological advances is important to you, find
an institution that offers these new services.

In the near future, your ATM card's capabilities, acceptance, and usefulness will probably be substantially ex-
panded. This is because your ATM card may soon be con-
verted into what is known as a point-of-sale debit card. This

change means that not only will your existing card still be
accepted at ATMs, but it can also be used at stores and
merchants that accept point-of-sale (POS) debit cards.

Two examples illustrate the types of activities that are
now occurring all across the country. First American Bank
in Washington, D.C. and Safeway recently initiated a program under which you can use your First American Money
Exchange card to pay for your groceries at Safeway. Working much like a credit card, you swipe your ATM card
through the reader in the Safeway checkout line, enter your
PIN, and your purchases are automatically debited on-line
from your banking account. Similarly, motorists in the Chicago area can now pay for gasoline, food items, and car repairs by using their Cash Station ATM cards at nearly five
hundred Amoco stations. Since payment by ATM is similar
to cash payment, Amoco customers who use their Cash Station card can still get the pricing breaks sometimes afforded
to cash customers.

Point-of-sale debit cards appear to be the wave of the
future. In fact, most of the major gasoline companies and
grocery store chains are already moving toward a nationwide system of point-of-sale terminals for their far-flung operations. Some national fast-food restaurant chains and
other retailers are not far behind. Smaller merchants are
starting to follow suit as well. As a result, these cards have
become far more widespread in recent years (especially on
the West Coast and in Europe). The coming months and
years should witness an explosion in the number of merchants accepting point-of-sale debit cards. With this antici-
pated expansion, your ATM card may soon be as widely accepted as a credit card is today.

Many people anticipate that debit cards will increasingly
replace checks as a payment device. And many financial in-

stitutions are aggressively working to see this happen. This is because the electronic funds transfers accomplished with debit cards are far less costly to them than handling a check, the processing of which is far more labor intensive.

Debit cards are better than checks in a number of ways. They are easier to carry. With a fully operational POS system, they will be more readily accepted out of town. They cost little or nothing to use; many are now offered for free. Most banks do not impose a monthly fee. While some currently assess transaction fees (a charge each time you use your debit card), these fees are lower than most ATM charges. The prevalence and size of debit transaction fees, however, may well increase as debit cards gain acceptance.

With debit cards, you are entitled to two types of records of your transaction: a receipt when the card is used and a monthly statement reflecting your debit card usage. These statements normally include the name of the person to whom or company to which payment was made. When writing a check, you do not get an automatic record of your transaction. In addition, most bank statements simply list the check number and no other identifying information, and may or may not provide you with canceled checks.

Debit cards have a couple of advantages over credit cards. Generally, no annual fees or interest rates are assessed on debit cards. However, it is entirely possible that once these point-of-sale systems become established and consumers start using them on a widespread basis, annual fees and/or transaction charges will be assessed. In fact, annual debit card fees are already under consideration by some issuers. Given this, check to see whether your issuer is charging an annual fee or transaction fees. If it is, make sure to factor these costs into your decision to use your debit card. You might also try to find a debit card issuer that does not charge such fees.

Debit cards also limit impulse buying to funds available in your account. Obviously, if you have overdraft protection and trigger it, you can still use a debit card up to the amount of your line of credit limit. In such an instance, you will be charged interest, thus significantly diminishing your savings with a debit card over a credit card.

There are both similarities and differences among checks, credit cards, and debit cards. With all three, you run the risk of being rejected at the sales counter when your transaction has been declined. With debit cards, you lose the "float" you enjoy with credit cards and checks. Some credit cards offer you a grace period of twenty-five to thirty days to pay your bill in full and avoid finance charges. With checks, there is normally a couple of days between when the check is written and when it is actually debited from your account. You do not get any float with debit cards. In fully functioning POS systems, funds may be immediately deducted from your account. Given this, make sure to keep track of your debit transactions and fees by writing them down in your checkbook ledger and deducting them from your balance.

❑ **Prepaid and Smart Cards**

In the future, American consumers will probably see increasing reliance upon "prepaid" and "smart" cards. If you've ever ridden the subway in the nation's Capital or used San Francisco's BART, you used a prepaid card. With these cards, for example, you exchange a $5 bill for a computer card with a dollar value of $5 that you then use within the subway system. Every time you exit the subway, the cost of your fare is deducted from your card. While in limited use today, such prepaid cards will probably become more prevalent in the future.

Smart cards are also currently being tested that will have a tiny computer microchip embedded in the plastic. This card will offer a wealth of services including personal information (such as medical histories) and bank account information (including every account you have with an institution). Using smart cards, consumers will be able to transfer funds, pay bills, utilize prepaid services, make airline reservations, purchase financial and other products, submit medical claims, and accomplish other sophisticated account transactions.

❑ Direct Deposits

Direct deposits allow you to designate specific recurring payments you may receive (payroll checks, Social Security benefits, pension, annuity, and other retirement checks, government assistance checks, dividends, and other similar payments) to be automatically deposited into your account on a regular basis. To avail yourself of this service, you must authorize these transactions in advance with the entity making the deposit. For example, you would sign up for deposit of your payroll check with your employer. You normally cannot authorize a direct deposit for a single payment you might receive (tax refunds are the big exception).

By arranging to have payments directly deposited, you receive funds more conveniently and securely. Since direct deposit is automatic, you still get paid on time even though you may be sick, out of town, away from work, or unable to get to the bank. Your checks cannot be lost or stolen in the mail, nor will they get held up by postal delays. Direct deposit also allows you to avoid long lines at teller windows on payday. Since you will not have to walk around with a pocketful of money, you do not have to worry about getting knocked over the head on your way home from the bank. You are also not subjected to the inconvenience and time delays of mailing in your deposits. Direct deposit may even give you earlier access to funds than regular paychecks. For example, employees with direct deposit may find their money available at the beginning of the day on payday while employees receiving paper checks have to wait until they are distributed to cash them. What's more, with direct deposit you never have to worry about a financial institution placing a hold on your check. The money is yours from the moment it is received by your institution. And if your money is directly deposited into an interest-bearing account, you start earning interest when your payment is received, not when you finally make it to the bank with your deposit.

Most financial institutions aggressively encourage you to use direct deposit. This is because direct deposit is a far cheaper and more efficient way for financial institutions to credit deposits to your account. Having to pay a teller to process your check and send it through the payments system costs them considerably more. Many financial institutions offer reduced-rate or free accounts to customers who use direct deposit. Check with several financial institutions in your area to see which ones offer such discounts. If you are willing to use direct deposit, you should be able to find a good deal from one of your local financial institutions. While most institutions do not charge for direct deposit, you should verify this just to make sure no charges are assessed.

Most financial institutions are able to accept direct deposit. Whether your employer, company, or agency that issues your checks makes payments by direct deposit varies. Many employers of different sizes use direct deposit. Some smaller employers may not. Similarly, some government benefits programs will not transmit benefits electronically as an abuse prevention device (they need to see their clients periodically and require that checks be picked up). If your employer or someone else from whom you receive payments does not currently offer direct deposit, ask them to consider using it. In some instances, employers and others may require you to use direct deposit to receive your payments. If this occurs, you are still free to select the institution to which the deposit is sent.

Federal, state, and local government benefits of the future may be transmitted via direct deposit as well. A number of experiments are currently under way in which food stamps, supplemental security income, and other government benefits payments are disbursed electronically instead of by paper check.

If you currently participate in the direct deposit program and experience problems because of a lost deposit or improper crediting of your account, you should complain both to the payer (your employer, Social Security, or whoever issued the check) and to your financial institution. Since some people experiencing direct deposit problems have complained that they get shuffled between their payer and their financial institution (they often blame each other for problems), complain to both at the outset. Specifically ask your financial institution to fill out a complaint form for transmittal to their regulator so government officials can accurately gauge the extent of deposit insurance problems.

While direct deposit has some definite advantages, it may not be appropriate for everyone. Some people simply prefer to conduct their financial business in person with paper checks. This is particularly true among older Americans and lower income persons. For example, roughly 18 million Social Security recipients refuse to use direct deposit (even though they have been subjected to aggressive marketing campaigns to enroll them in this service). Financial institutions would like nothing better than to require the use of di-

rect deposit as a necessary precondition for obtaining any
banking services. Since different people have different
needs, consumers will hopefully still be able to choose between whether to use direct deposit or to receive their payments by paper check. If having this choice is important to
you, do not let financial institutions and others talk you into
using direct deposit if you are uncomfortable with it. In
most cases, you are still entitled to receive your payments
by paper check if you so desire.

❑ **Automatic Direct Withdrawals/Electronic Payments**
    Automatic direct withdrawals/electronic payments are a
convenient and efficient way of handling routine payments
(like loan and mortgage payments, insurance premiums, util-
ity bills, charitable deductions, savings deposits). In banking
circles, these services are also known as pre-authorized deb-
its. Because you do not have to write checks, this simplifies
your monthly financial chores. You will have fewer checks
to write and fewer stamps to lick for each payment that is
handled automatically. You spend less time paying bills and
enjoy reduced postage costs. In fact, the average savings on
stamps alone for a consumer who mails in ten to fifteen
checks per month is $35 to $52 a year! What's more, automatically making your payments assures that they will be
credited on time, as scheduled each month. Thus, you will
avoid late payment penalties. Should you forget about a
payment or be tied up somewhere else, your payments will
occur automatically. You do not have to lift a finger.
    With automatic payments, funds are automatically deb-
ited from your bank account on the same date each month
and applied to your outstanding loan balance, savings account, etc. Quite often you can choose the date a withdrawal is to occur each month. Automatic payments can be

used for your monthly bills that are constant (for example, your monthly $750 mortgage payment) or variable (for example, your monthly telephone bill, the dollar amount of which fluctuates each month). Make sure to include these payments in your bank account ledger and to deduct the amount from your account balance. When using direct withdrawals/electronic payments, you must make absolutely certain that the required amount of money will always be in your account each month on the date when the payment is due. If the money's not there, you could overdraft your account.

Like direct deposit, you must specifically authorize these payment transactions in advance with the company withdrawing money from your account. For example, you decide to use automatic payments to have a certain amount of money withdrawn from your checking account each month and placed into a mutual fund account. This can be done whether you purchase this mutual fund from your own bank or from a mutual fund company across the country. This is a standing authorization which remains in effect until you revoke it (which can be done at any time). While most financial institutions offer automatic payments, some companies and vendors may not. For example, your landlord may insist upon a paper check each month.

By using automatic payments, you may also qualify for a lower interest rate on a new loan. For example, suppose you take out a new-car loan at your financial institution. If you are willing to authorize direct payments out of your account to repay this loan, you may get the interest rate on the loan reduced by as much as a full percentage point. This is because your financial institution's administrative costs are reduced. So if you are considering a new loan, see which financial institutions in your local area discount for automatic bill payments. It may be well worth your while to get your loan from an institution that discounts, even though you may have to move your banking account to this institution in order to qualify.

There is normally no charge for automatic payments. Some institutions, however, assess transaction charges for automatic payments that are sent outside of your institution. Given this, make sure to check on your institution's policy before committing to payments whose costs will be increased because of such charges.

❑ **Telephone Bill Payment Services**

Many financial institutions offer specialized telephone bill payment services that permit you to pay all kinds of bills by telephone. In contrast to the automatic payments discussed above, telephone bill payment services require you to take action every time a payment is made. This does not happen automatically.

If you opt for this service, you must first complete an authorization form and provide a list of payees. The offering institution will then normally send you a verification statement, numerical codes for your payees, an account number, and a numerical secret code. To pay bills, you must call the bill payment telephone number, dial the account number and secret code, then enter each payee code and payment amount.

While services vary with provider, customers are often able to authorize individual payments by telephone on regular monthly payments for rent, utilities, credit cards, loans, mortgage payments, and other continuing obligations. The charge for this service may be less than the cost of postage. Some institutions even offer it for free to customers who use direct deposit or maintain balances in excess of a certain amount. Per-transaction fees may be assessed if you pay more than the allowable number of bills in any given month.

Many telephone bill payment services operate twenty-four hours a day, seven days a week. Some even offer a toll-free number so you can make payments from out of town. These services are offered using live operators or automated voice response systems. As for the future, new devices are currently under development that will facilitate bill payment through screen-based telephones, hand-held computers, and interactive television.

Some financial institutions already offer special screen-based telephones that can be used for a variety of activities. For example, Citibank's "Enhanced Telephone" allows customers to access account information, transfer money between accounts, pay bills electronically, buy CDs and mutual funds, and conduct a myriad of other activities. These telephones, which are available on a limited basis in select markets, normally have a small screen that can accommodate anywhere from one to forty lines of text. These devices may well become "mini ATMs" for the home (except that they obviously will not dispense cash). Fees for such special telephone services range from $10 to $20 per month.

❏ Account Information Telephone Lines

Many financial institutions now provide easy access to account information over the telephone. These services allow you to bank on your own schedule (not just when the bank is open). Some account information lines have live consumer service representatives offering personalized service relating to a variety of your banking needs. These are usually staffed during regular business hours (although some, like Citibank, are staffed around the clock). Others offer computerized telephone information systems which operate hours a day; some have more limited hours. While most use local numbers, many also have toll-free numbers

so you can easily access account information while you are
away from home.

Using a touch-tone telephone, you simply dial a special
number and enter your access code. Many financial institutions require you to use an ATM card and your assigned
personal identification number (PIN) to access your account. Account information telephone lines are generally
available to all customers with ATM cards. No separate registration beyond getting the ATM is required. Access to
these account information lines is often free. They are provided as a customer convenience by most financial institutions.

While systems vary among institutions, once you get
into the system, many allow you to access all sorts of information and services, including: checking your account balance, determining which checks have been paid, getting the
date and amount of your most recent deposits, obtaining
your interest earnings last year on your savings and investment accounts, transferring money between accounts, paying certain bills (credit card and loan repayments at the
bank), stopping payment of checks, and reordering checks.
Many of these also offer access to information about current
lending rates, other accounts, and assorted services.

Many credit card issuers offer "800" services to access
credit card account information as well. Some institutions
even allow you to ask for increases in your line of credit
over the telephone. Sometimes approvals are given while
you wait or you will be advised of the decision within a matter of hours. Some financial institutions also offer "loan by
phone" services for applying for installment and other loans.

❏ Home Banking by Computer Services
The purchase by millions of Americans of home computers now permits many people to do much of their bank-

ing from home. With a modem and a telephone, you can easily link your computer up to one at your bank so the two can "converse" through telephone lines (provided your bank offers this service). Unlike some of the automatic transmittal services mentioned below, home banking by computer services are interactive. This means that you are talking directly to your bank's computer rather than directing others to make payments from your accounts. Home banking by computer offers you timely information about your accounts and enables you to conduct some of your banking business much more conveniently.

Home banking by computer services are not available at all financial institutions. Those offering this service require you to sign up before accessing it. Once you have done this, you dial a special telephone number to reach your bank's computer. At a prompt, you key in appropriate identifying information (like your account number, ATM card number, or your PIN). You can then read messages from the bank on your screen and punch in instructions to accomplish an array of banking activities. The specific features of different services vary considerably. Most permit you to check account balances, learn which checks and deposits have cleared, transfer funds between accounts, and pay bills.

Charges and services vary. Many of these home banking by computer services charge a fee of about $10 a month for a select number of transactions. Additional fees for transactions in excess of the allowable number will then be assessed. Since home banking is available only to those with a personal computer, the expense of the computer and modem must also be taken into consideration.

❑ **Dedicated Terminals**
A handful of financial institutions across the country

have been test-marketing dedicated banking terminals.
These terminals, which are maintained by consumers in their
homes or offices, access the institution's computer system.
Once on-line, consumers utilize twenty-four or more lines of
video text to accomplish banking transactions. The terminals are hard-wired to the bank and cannot be used for other
purposes. Since these devices, which can either be purchased or leased, are only being used in test markets, cost
figures are not available. While some dedicated terminals
are still available on a limited basis, most financial institutions are moving away from these single-function devices.

❑ **Television Banking**
Some observers think we will be using our television
sets to conduct banking services in the years ahead. Computer software and related materials are currently being
tested that would allow you to access banking accounts
through your telephone or a special keypad. Account information and other transactions that can be done on an ATM
(except obtaining cash) would then appear on your television screen. Costs for such services are not yet known.

❑ **Wire Transfers**
Through what is known as a wire transfer, you can
move money from most financial institutions to anywhere in
the United States and to many foreign countries. Once this
money arrives at the financial institution on the other end, it
can either be deposited into the recipient's account or paid
directly to the recipient by the institution. Wire transfers,
which sometimes carry hefty minimum fees, are most often
used for the transfer of large amounts of money. They can,
however, still be used for smaller amounts, but only if the
cost of the service can be justified.

To accomplish a wire transfer, you simply complete a funds transfer form at your local financial institution and pay the required wire transfer fee. In some instances, the recipient will also be charged a wire transfer fee from the receiving institution. Since pricing policies vary, check with your local institution. Some will waive or reduce wire transfer fees for certain customers.

Your Rights Under the Electronic Funds Transfer Act

❑ **Required Disclosures**
Disclosures When Registering for the Service. When you register for any services that involve electronic funds transfers, you must be given documents explaining your legal rights and responsibilities. This is required under the federal Electronic Funds Transfer Act. Before you contract for EFT services or conduct your first EFT transaction, the issuing institution is required to give you documents containing the following information.

○ A summary of your liability for unauthorized transfers

○ The telephone number and address of the person to be notified when an unauthorized transfer has been or may be made

○ The type of transfers you can make, the amount of any charges for transfers, and any limitations on the frequency and dollar amount of transfers

○ A summary of your right to receive documentation of transfers, your right to stop-payment on a pre-authorized transfer, and stop-payment procedures

O A notice describing the procedures you must follow to
   report an error on an EFT receipt, how to request more
   information about a transfer listed on your statement,
   and the time period in which you must make your report

O A summary of the institution's liability if it fails to make
   or stop certain transactions

   Disclosures for Each Transaction. In addition to the
disclosures you receive upon signing up for an EFT service,
you should also receive the following two types of notices
for each EFT transaction you accomplish.

O Terminal receipt (a record of your transaction)

O Periodic statement (for each statement cycle in which an
   EFT transaction is made)

You should keep and compare your EFT receipts with the
transactions listed on your statement. This should enable
you to spot errors and correct them promptly.

❑ **EFT Fraud**
         The recommendations in chapter 9 on credit and
charge card fraud are equally applicable to protecting you
against EFT fraud. For EFT cards, keep the following additional recommendations in mind.

O Do not write your personal identification number (PIN)
   on your EFT card or on anything else you keep in your
   wallet or pocketbook. You might select a PIN that cor-
   responds to a familiar name. Some people hide their PIN
   under a dummy name among listings in an address book

(with the first or last several digits of a street address or a telephone number reflecting the PIN number).

O Select a PIN that is different from other numbers that may be present in your wallet or pocketbook (such as your birth date, address, telephone number, or Social Security number).

O Memorize your PIN.

O Never give your PIN to anyone else.

O Be careful not to allow anyone to discover your PIN through watching your EFT card use.

O Immediately examine all EFT receipts and statements. If EFT fraud occurs, your rights are as follows:

O If you report your EFT card missing before it is used without your permission, you are not responsible for any unauthorized use of the card.

O If an unauthorized use occurs and you report the card missing within two business days after you notice its loss, your maximum liability cannot exceed $50.

O If an unauthorized use occurs and you do not report the card missing within two business days after you notice its loss, your maximum liability jumps to $500.

O If an unauthorized use occurs and you do not report the card missing within sixty days after your bank statement is mailed to you, you could lose all your remaining balance in the account, along with any available overdraft protection you may have attached to your account.

Since your out-of-pocket expenses are reduced through the earliest notification of your financial institution, contact them immediately upon learning of the loss. Remember, once you report the loss of your EFT card, you cannot be held responsible for any future unauthorized transactions.

❑ Correcting Errors

You have sixty days from the date a problem or error appears on your terminal receipt or periodic statement to notify your financial institution. If you find an error, send your issuer a letter (certified, return receipt requested). Keep a copy for your records. Upon receipt of your letter, the institution has ten business days to investigate and advise you of the results of its investigation. If the institution needs more time, it can take up to forty-five days to investigate and report to you (but not without temporarily returning the amount of the dispute in question to your account). At the end of the investigation, the institution may reclaim this money (if no error is found), provided it sends you a written explanation.

If you fail to notify your institution of an error within sixty days, it is under no legal obligation to investigate. So if you find EFT errors, let your institution know immediately.

Electronic Services Available from Others

❑ Computer Software Offerings

A lot of new personal financial management computer software has come on the market in recent years. Most of these programs enable you to keep track of banking activities, balance your checkbook, compute interest earnings and credit costs, develop budgets, see graphic visualizations of your spending and savings practices, remind you of recurring payments, conduct tax and financial planning sessions, and accomplish a variety of other financial tasks on your computer. If you are interested in some of these popular, state-of-the-art financial management software packages, consider the following: Balance Point, CheckFree, Cheque-It-Out, Managing Your Money, Microsoft Money, MoneyCounts, Quicken, and WinCheck. Software prices range from $20 to $100. There are considerable differences in these packages and what they offer. To learn more about this financial management software, consult the January 12, 1993, edition of *PC Magazine*, which contains a sixteen-page critique of these programs.

If you only want to keep your bank account ledger, reconcile balances, and pay your bills electronically, you do not need the above financial management software. You can do this directly by purchasing CheckFree's basic software and subscribing to its bill payment service. Here is how CheckFree works. You enter your initial payment information "off-line" into your personal computer using the CheckFree software or the CheckFree-capable versions of Managing Your Money or Quicken. Then, with your computer and modem, you get "on-line" by dialing either an assigned local number or an 800 number and using your account code to have your bills paid. Monthly payments can be made in one of two ways. You can have recurring payments automatically sent each month. Or payments will be made only after you send a payment command to CheckFree. Upon receipt, payments will be made electronically or mailed to your identified creditors (if an electronic transmittal cannot be made). For example, your paperboy does not yet accept electronic payments. This process makes certain your payments arrive at their destinations on time. It also saves you the time and trouble of addressing, stamping, and licking envelopes each month.

CheckFree's software retails for about $30. The monthly charge for the first twenty payments is around $10, while additional blocks of payments are available for a modest additional fee. If you are on the CompuServe computer network, you can also access CheckFree. However, in addition to your regular CompuServe fee, you will also be required to pay CheckFree's monthly fee.

Similar services exist from other providers. For example, PRODIGY and BillPay USA are linked up to allow customers to accomplish electronic bill payments. Again, the cost of BillPay USA, which is comparable to CheckFree, is in addition to the PRODIGY service membership fee.

❑ **Telephone and Consumer Electronics Company Offerings**

A number of telephone and consumer electronics companies are now offering or will soon start offering new-generation home telephones that can electronically accomplish a host of activities. These products are separate and apart from the services mentioned above which are sometimes available through financial institutions. For a monthly charge of $10 to $25, you will be allowed to buy groceries, balance your checkbook, and pay your bills—all from the convenience of your home. Services and hardware vary. Some of these new telephones have a slot into which you can insert a credit or debit card to pay for your purchases (in much the same fashion that credit card purchases are now verified by merchants). Some offer an electronic light wand that can be used to scan a listing of bar codes for your various bills and shopping needs. These souped-up telephones usually have a small screen (with one to four lines of text) that flashes instructions to guide you through transactions. These services do not require you to have a home computer. Since these telephones are part of an "information services" outreach that many telephone and consumer electronics companies are now moving into, you can expect to see similar new services coming on the market with increasing frequency.

❑ **Your Rights Concerning Computer Software, Telephone and Consumer Electronics Company Services**

You may not be entitled to any specific legal protections when you avail yourself of the computer software, telephone and consumer electronics company services mentioned in the last several pages. It is unclear at this point whether the federal Electronic Funds Transfer Act even applies to these types of activities. However, should problems arise, you may be entitled to protection under state law. You might also send letters of complaint to both the Federal Trade Commission (FTC) and the Federal Communications Commission (FCC), alerting them to problems you may be experiencing. The FTC's and FCC's addresses are as follow.

Federal Trade Commission
Credit Practices Division
6th & Pennsylvania Aves., NW
Washington, DC 20580

Federal Communications
　Commission
1919 M St., NW
Washington, DC 20554

RECOMMENDATIONS

There are a lot of electronic banking services available to help you accomplish your banking activities. These will enable you to streamline your financial management duties, eliminate unnecessary time and effort spent on financial chores, enhance your personal safety, and help you to shop around for the best financial products available. If you're not currently using some of these services, you should learn more about them and seriously consider using them.

The financial services marketplace of the future is going to be dramatically different from the one to which you may be accustomed. Soon your ATM card will be as widely accepted by different merchants and business establishments as your credit card is today. Many people are already benefiting from new debit technologies.

If you have a personal computer, you can also pay your bills electronically from home without ever licking a stamp or mailing an envelope. Certain computer software programs allow you to accomplish a host of financial activities from the comfort of your home.

12

Resolving Banking Complaints

Cyndie is having a problem with her bank and doesn't know where to turn. In spite of repeated complaints to the bank directly, the problem has still not been resolved to her satisfaction. Cyndie has a variety of options available to assert her rights and to get the bank to respond to her problem.

You are entitled to access to information, specific legal rights, and protection against certain abusive practices under the federal consumer statutes. If you wish to enforce your rights under any of these statutes or the regulations that implement them, your options are listed below.

How and Where to Complain

❑ First Complain to Your Financial Services Provider

You should first complain directly to the financial services provider against which you have a complaint. Go directly to the unit involved. If it was a bank branch, talk to the manager. If it was the credit card department, contact its director. In verbal communications with financial provider employees, speak calmly but firmly. Above all, be persistent. Do not let them pass the buck or ignore you. If you are not satisfied with responses, jot down names and titles.

If contacting a branch or department does not speedily resolve your problem, do not rely on the decisions of subordinates. Go immediately to the top. Find out the name and address of an officer or the person in charge and send your complaint to that person. If it is a large organization, appeal to the head of the department, the divisional manager, or the president of the company.

At this point, put your complaint in writing. In your letter, make sure to present your version of the situation and why you feel a complaint is necessary. Identify both your problem and the remedy you seek. If you believe a federal law or regulation has been violated, make it clear that you are aware of the law. Give the financial service provider your preferred resolution of the problem as well as a prioritized listing of options that might also resolve the conflict. Ask for a prompt response by a certain date (for example, within two weeks). Indicate in your letter that you are attempting to resolve the matter directly with the financial services provider. However, you will be left with no other alternative but to complain to their regulator if they fail to make a good-faith effort to work with you toward resolution. If the officer you contact fails to reply by the deadline you have set, send a follow-up letter, call to check on the status of your complaint, or file a complaint with the appropriate federal regulatory agency. Keep copies of all correspondence for your files and possible further use.

In many cases, your complaint will be referred by higher-ups back to the first unit you contacted. But this time it will probably get the attention it deserves. If things are not resolved to your satisfaction after the second go-around, call the bank officer again to let him or her know you still have a problem.

❑ Complain to the Appropriate Federal Regulatory Agency

Before complaining about your financial services provider to a federal regulatory agency, you first need to determine which federal regulatory agency has jurisdiction. Ask your financial services provider for the name, address, and telephone number of this agency. You can also determine the appropriate federal regulatory agency from the information provided below.

Type of Financial Services Provider	Where to Complain
Nationally chartered bank ("National" or "NA" will appear in name)	Comptroller of the Currency Consumer Activities Division 250 E St., SW Washington, DC 20219
State-chartered bank (FDIC-insured and a member of Federal Reserve System)	Federal Reserve Board Division of Consumer & Community Affairs 20th & Constitution Aves., NW Washington, DC 20551

<u>Type of Financial Services Provider</u>	<u>Where to Complain</u>
State-chartered bank (FDIC-insured but not a member of Federal Reserve System)	Federal Deposit Insurance Corp. Office of Consumer Affairs 550 17th St., NW Washington, DC 20429
Federally chartered or insured savings and loan association	Office of Thrift Supervision Consumer Affairs 1700 G St., NW Washington, DC 20552
Federally chartered credit union ("Federal Credit Union" appears in the name)	Natl. Credit Union Administration 1776 G St., NW Washington, DC 20456
State-chartered credit union, finance company, charge card company, retail or department store, credit-reporting agency, public utility company, government lending program, state-chartered banks or savings institutions without FDIC insurance	Federal Trade Commission Bureau of Consumer Protection Office of Credit Practices Sixth and Pennsylvania, NW Washington, DC 20580

Direct your letter of complaint to the appropriate agency. You might consider mailing a copy of the letter you send to the federal regulatory agency to the institution against which you are lodging the complaint. If the institution knows you are taking your complaint to a higher authority, it may be more willing to accommodate your request.

A complaint to a federal regulatory agency must be in writing. When filing a complaint, give as much information as possible explaining your side of the story, including specific details (dates and times, your activities, company responses, names of persons with whom you have spoken, etc.). Send along copies of any relevant materials (letters you have sent or received, copies of account or loan documents, etc.).

Since federal regulatory agencies are not responsible for resolving individual cases, do not expect them to intercede on your behalf once they receive your complaint. Your complaint will be grouped with other consumer complaints and investigated. Your complaint, along with others, may alert the agency to a violation of a federal consumer statute. These complaints might help the agency determine if a pattern of practice exists (for example, a particular institution has been violating the law with respect to other people as well). Armed with the information you provide, examiners will scrutinize an institution in the area of your complaint on their next visit.

❏ Contact Local News Organizations and Consumer Organizations

If you think your gripe with a particular financial institution is something other customers are being subjected to, contact local media representatives to see if they might be enticed to do a story on the problem. Negative publicity is something most institutions will try to avoid at all costs. In addition, if the problem is fairly widespread, contact local consumer organizations that handle consumer complaints to see if they will get involved. To have a local advocacy group squawking about your problem would add fuel to the fire and might prompt the institution to respond favorably.

❏ Sue in Federal Court

If you wish to pursue legal action, consult with an attorney about bringing a suit in federal court against your financial services provider. You can usually either bring a suit in your own right or participate in a class-action suit. While it may not be worth your while to pursue legal action over a $5 dispute, a class-action suit (where you are joined by other people who have been subjected to the same practice) may be more appropriate.

❏ **Pursue State and Local Actions**

You may also be protected under a state law, as some states have enacted laws to protect their citizens concerning certain consumer financial transactions. Consult with a local attorney to see if your state has enacted such a law. If so, you should be able to file a complaint with the appropriate state agency (such as the state banking commission, state and local consumer protection agencies, state attorney general's office). You might also try contacting the local Better Business Bureau. In addition, you may be able to sue in a state court. Again, check with a local attorney to see whether this is possible.

❏ **Avoid Binding, Mandatory Arbitration**

Some financial institutions have initiated policies that force consumers to use binding, mandatory arbitration in lieu of a court trial when resolving disputes involving their accounts (checking, savings, and credit card accounts). Such actions rob consumers of important legal protections.

For example, in the summer of 1992, Bank of America (now the nation's second largest bank) announced that it was unilaterally requiring the use of arbitration for its consumer accounts. The company asserted that language in existing consumer account agreements gives it broad latitude in changing the terms of such agreements. No approval on the part of Bank of America's millions of unsuspecting customers was required. Mere use of an account implies the customer's acceptance of the revised terms. Consumers were informed of the change with a small-type notice included in monthly bank and credit card statements. A couple of weeks after Bank of America foisted arbitration upon its customers, Wells Fargo (another large financial institution) followed suit. Bank of America's scheme prohibits customers from pursing any legal actions; small-claims court actions are not even allowed. Wells Fargo's plan only limits access to the courts where $25,000 or more is at stake. It is feared that increasing numbers of financial institutions will follow Bank of America's lead and will soon implement binding, mandatory arbitration practices.

Similar to a trial, arbitration is a closed-door proceeding conducted before a referee, often a retired judge. Some consumer advocates question the impartiality of the referees who are frequently called upon by the banks for this purpose. What's more, unlike a trial, you are not entitled to a jury of your peers and may be unable to appeal an adverse ruling.

The financial institutions that require binding, mandatory arbitration are attempting to contain legal costs in defending lawsuits brought by consumers and consumer group representatives. These cases—some of them successful—have contested exorbitant returned-check charges, challenged credit card interest rate price-fixing practices, questioned the legality of late fees, and otherwise sought to protect consumers against abusive financial institution practices.

Check your existing account paperwork carefully. Be on the lookout for innocuous disclosures in your monthly bills that may substantially change your rights. Try to avoid doing business with financial institutions that require you to give up your legal rights in exchange for arbitration. You may have a problem if most of the financial services providers in your area require the use of arbitration or if you live in a rural area where your only local bank has started this practice. If this is the case, let the bank president know that you are opposed to this language and ask that its arbitration policy be reevaluated. Maybe they will even be willing to strike the offending language from your contract or not make it applicable to you. In addition, alert local reporters and consumer organizations to the issue and encourage them to become involved. Some Bank of America customers and consumer groups in California have filed suit against the financial services giant questioning the legality of its new arbitration policy.

RECOMMENDATIONS

If you are having problems with a financial institution, you need to assert your rights. This should start with complaining directly to the financial institution. Then, if the problem is not resolved to your satisfaction, file a complaint with the institution's governmental regulator. To focus attention upon your problem, consider contacting local news and consumer organizations to alert them to your complaint. If you feel that you have a strong case, you might consider suing in state or federal court. Wherever possible, avoid financial institutions that require you to use binding, mandatory arbitration.

Index